From Workout to Last Call

A PRACTICAL GUIDE TO NETWORKING, INCREASING SOCIAL CAPITAL AND SUCCEEDING AT EVENTS, TRADE SHOWS, AND CONFERENCES

PAUL ABDOOL

Published in Canada by Handshake Press

paulabdool.ca

FROM WORKOUT TO LAST CALL:
A Practical Guide To Networking, Increasing Social Capital And Succeeding At Events, Trade Shows, And Conferences

Trade Paper: 978-1-77168-434-7

Published in Canada
Printed in United States of America

1. BUSINESS & ECONOMICS / Business Communication / Meetings & Presentations

2. BUSINESS & ECONOMICS / Careers / Career Advancement & Professional Development

Contents

For those who embrace challenges,

even when they feel uncertain or afraid.

Introduction

Trade shows and conferences often provoke mixed reactions. While some people perceive them as essential investments, others dismiss them as wasteful extravagances or even a boondoggle. The truth lies somewhere in between in the real world.

Success at these events is not guaranteed — it requires careful planning, meticulous organization and dedicated effort or it will not be fruitful.

Having experienced the full spectrum of outcomes firsthand, I have come to appreciate the importance of a strategic and energetic approach. In this guide, I'll share insights gained from years of navigating the highs and lows of trade shows, conferences and events.

This book is full of street-level insights and "Pro Tips" that can transform your mindset and approach to these events. From pre-event preparation to on-the-ground execution, and from navigating the chaos of the show floor and networking sessions to the post-event follow-ups, I explore the keys to maximizing your own and your company's investment to reap the rewards of these opportunities.

From Workout to Last Call is analogous to always being ready to represent you and your company. The concept is simple: if you are awake, you should be "working." When I say working, I'm not saying you should always be selling or pitching, but you should be ready to network by showing up from sunrise to the last opportunity to converse with someone.

Yes, it is exhausting.

Yes, you can do it, regardless of whether you're an extravert, an introvert or an ambivert.

Yes, you will leave tired.

So, how do you go about doing this?

Read on to master the art and science of turning an event or conference from a potential waste of money into a powerful opportunity for your company and your personal brand.

Show up ... *From Workout to Last Call* ... and hustle!

Paul Abdool

1

The Why

Why should you even bother networking or attending a conference, trade show or event?[1]

Social capital!

Social capital refers to the resources and benefits that individuals or groups gain through their networks of relationships.

These resources include:

- Trust
- Information
- Influence
- Support
- Cooperation

These resources can enhance personal and professional success. Social capital relies on mutual connections and shared norms within a network or community, making it valuable for gaining access to new opportunities, acquiring knowledge and strengthening social cohesion.

According to Nahapiet and Ghoshal's[2] definition:

Social capital is "the sum of the actual and potential resources embedded within, available through, and derived from the network of relationships possessed by an individual or social unit. Social capital thus comprises both the network and the assets that may be mobilized through that network."

Others elaborate on social capital, dividing it into three types[3] [4]:

1. **Bonding social capital**: This type arises from close-knit relationships, such as family and close friends. It reinforces trust, loyalty and emotional support but can sometimes be exclusive or inward-focused.

---

[1] For the sake of simplicity, I will use the word "event" to represent all references to events, trade shows or conferences, unless I am specifically talking about one in particular.

[2] Nahapiet, Janine, and Sumantra Ghoshal. 1998. "Social capital, intellectual capital, and the organizational advantage." Academy of Management Review 23: 242.

[3] Social capital: https://www.socialcapitalresearch.com/wp-content/uploads/2018/11/Functions-of-Social-Capital.pdf

[4] Robert Putnam, *Bowling Alone*

2. **Bridging social capital**: This type is derived from more distant, diverse connections that link individuals or groups across different social or professional circles. It provides access to broader opportunities, novel information, and resources outside one's immediate community.

3. **Linking social capital**: This form connects people to institutions or individuals in positions of authority, often facilitating access to resources, services or power.

Social capital is a dynamic, intangible asset, as it is built and maintained through continuous interaction, trust and reciprocity within a network.

** Pro Tip – Social Capital = Job Insurance **

In my opinion, social capital is equal to job insurance.

All of my jobs in the past 25 years have come from networking and increasing my social capital. As Dave Delaney, founder and CEO of Futureforth, says, "Everyone should build their network before they need it."[5]

According to the LinkedIn Opportunity Index 2020[6], "The significance of professional networks is generally overlooked. We find respondents' attitudes towards professional networks interesting … 76% of our respondents believe knowing the right people is key to getting ahead but only 22% are actively seeking networking opportunities."

For simplicity and clarity, this book is broken into two very connected sections:

1. Event Execution
2. Networking Nexus

Events are where people are.

Networking cannot be done without other people.

Your networking and social capital begin with interactions, usually in person, usually at events.

The rest is up to you and your efforts. Don't just phone it in … event success takes effort and requires thoughtful planning and logistics.

---

[5] https://www.davedelaney.me/

[6] https://business.linkedin.com/content/dam/me/business/en-us/talent-solutions/emerging-jobs-report/pdf/LinkedIn-Opportunity-Index-2020-Global.pdf

All Pro Tips throughout the book can
be found in the Pro Tips Index.

SECTION 1 – EVENT EXECUTION

Chapter 1 – Getting Started

Where do I start?

Should I even go to an event?

Is it worth it?

Am I ready?

Do I have the money?

What should my message be?

What would I say to people?

These are all great questions and real things to deal with before embarking on your journey. Like any journey, you should have a starting point and destination. The destination does not have to be fully defined, but you should have a solid idea or hypothesis prior to embarkation. My assumption is that you will need some budget, and you may not be funding 100% of it by yourself. Or if you are, it may be even more important to know where you are headed.

Let's embark on your destination.

What are you trying to accomplish?

Businesses:

The answer to the question could be brand exposure or recognition, building a pipeline for your business or sales team, entering a new market, or all of the above.

Individuals:

The answer could be learning more about your industry or a new market, achieving a certification, speaking, or networking for your business or for your professional future.

By the way, you can accomplish both business and personal goals at a single event. If you grow, your business grows. It is not selfish; it is an outcome. The personal growth elements will be peppered within the business growth elements because they do not operate independently; they are both part of the overall recipe for success.

7

If you were chosen for an event mission, appreciate why you were chosen or provided the resources to participate. It could change your life.

You may meet the person that can help you develop the skills that will elevate you or your company. That person or group may be able to introduce you to a person that can help you raise your personal network capital or take your company to the next level. Embrace the challenge and accept that you will not be perfect.

I promise you that you will be better for showing up and participating.

Market Research

Now that you have contemplated your "Why?", which events, conferences or trade shows should you attend?

How do you know if the event is right for you and your organization?

What other organizations are going to be there?

These are just a few of the questions that you will be asked by the person that owns the budget for events. This budget owner may even be you. Essentially, you are all trying to establish from a qualitative perspective if you or the company should attend. Inevitably the next logical step, soon thereafter, is to migrate into the quantitative discussion.

Some common budget owner questions are:

- How much is it?
- When is it?
- Do you think we will get anything out of it … as in, new business and revenue?

Typically, show budgets range from $5,000 to $100,000.

The cost range depends on several factors, including the size and prestige of the show, booth size, location on the floor, booth design, shipping and setup, staff and travel expenses, and promotional activities before and after the event.

The management team and accountants maintain a steadfast focus on the bottom line, so you better have answers to their questions. The good news is, this book will provide the tools so you can calculate the answers and provide insights into why you should attend and what you can expect if you execute properly. See Return on Event (ROE) section for more information and equations.

See Appendix A – Business Cases

- Trade Show Business Case
- Attendee Business Case

Please note, although a positive financial outcome is important, networking and events are not always *transactional*. Networking is not meant to be 100% transactional.

Remember the definition of Social Capital:

- Social capital is "the sum of the actual and potential resources embedded within, available through, and derived from the network of relationships possessed by an individual or social unit. Social capital thus comprises both the network and the assets that may be mobilized through that network."

So, what should you look for in a good event?

Everyone wants to have meaningful conversations and make connections. The environment must be right to attract key players in the ecosystem: customers/prospects, industry professionals, partners, service providers and vendors.

As a rule, there are some elements that make an event attractive to the ecosystem:

- Location
- Cost
- Themes or subject matter
- Potential business opportunities versus opportunity costs
- Timing or seasonality
- The Experience Factor ("je ne sais quoi")[7]
  - An almost indescribable component of an event that goes beyond its transactional purpose (e.g., buying, selling, or learning) to create emotional engagement and memorable moments that bring people back

---

[7] English translation from French: "I don't know what"

- The "Bump" Factor
  - The busy bustle and energy of an event, mixed with the pleasant experience of bumping into people at an event, can often create a mix of spontaneity, connection and unexpected delight. (See Figure 1 – The Bump Factor)

Figure 1 – The Bump Factor

Some events have a reputation for being the "go-to event" — everybody goes there for one reason or another. Sometimes you do not know where these hidden gems are, unless you have been in the industry for a long time; sometimes it is blatantly obvious.

There are a few questions to ask yourself.

- Are your competitors there?
- Do you want to go where "everyone" is?
- Do you want to go against the stream or take a shot at a potential blue ocean?

Distinguishing between Horizontal and Vertical events can sometimes support your decisions. The definition of these and what they set out to accomplish may provide some clarity.

Horizontal (Ecosystem) Trade Show or Event

Definition:

- A horizontal B2B (business-to-business) trade show or event with an exhibition that brings together businesses from multiple industries or sectors to showcase products, services and solutions.
- Examples: Shoptalk, SXSW (South by Southwest), PACK EXPO International

Cross-industry focus:

- Exhibitors represent diverse sectors such as technology, manufacturing, logistics, retail, healthcare, and finance, creating opportunities for businesses to explore solutions beyond their immediate industry.
- Expand and broaden your thinking ... get out of the echo chamber of a community that is always saying the same things.

Diverse solutions and offerings:

- Exhibitors present a variety of B2B solutions, such as software platforms, industrial tools, supply chain technologies, and consulting services, catering to the needs of businesses across sectors.

Focus on universal business challenges:

- Sessions, panels and demonstrations often address common business themes, such as digital transformation, cost optimization, sustainability, and leadership, which are relevant to businesses regardless of their sector.

Questions:

- Do you go where everyone is?
- Will you be lost in the sea of vendors and people?

Your company could be the only provider in your category, which can be both good and bad. Good because you have no competition, but bad because the attendees may not be in market for what you are selling.

Here are a few examples.

A system integrator may attend a retail show because they know that large companies will be there that use a large tech stack. However, there may not be a lot of technical people there to appreciate your offering. On the other hand, the business owner that is frustrated with disconnected experiences may connect the dots and schedule a meeting with the committee looking into these challenges.

Another example: Your firm may implement some sort of technology that attending firms may use, but it is not core to their business. Address correction software at a financial/banking show may be very important to these people because bills are not being paid, or they are losing customers when they move.

Vertical Trade Show or Events

Definition:

A vertical B2B trade show is a specialized exhibition that focuses on a single industry, sector or niche, bringing together businesses that operate within the same market.

Industry-specific focus:

- Exhibitors and attendees are concentrated within a single industry, such as automotive, healthcare, construction or aerospace, fostering a highly relevant and focused environment.

Specialized products and solutions:

- Exhibitors showcase industry-specific products, services and technologies tailored to meet the unique needs of businesses within the sector.

Industry-specific knowledge sharing:

- Educational sessions, keynote speeches, and workshops address challenges, trends and advancements that are unique to the industry, providing actionable insights for professionals.

Questions:

- Do you have the data that suggests you should focus on a particular vertical market?
- Are your customers and partners expecting you to be there?
- Is it time to take your product to a different region or market?

You may believe that your product or service should be used by a particular market segment that has not been fully explored. You may have one or two customers in that segment, but your marketing team has not exploited it yet. This may be the opportunity to turn up the heat and expand this market before others find your "quiet island" that is rich in potential business and revenue.

Typically, your competitors and partners are present at vertical events because there are a few "must attend" nexus events each year that the market is drawn to.

This is a central marketplace. It is the same reason why furniture or lighting stores gather in a certain area. This collocated cluster makes it easier for customers that are in market to compare and contrast options in real time. It also can draw more foot traffic to a particular zone at a show (e.g., start-up zone, e-commerce zone). In some cases, competitors are placed in a head-to-head arena, like a mini-sales-pitch segment of the event or as part of an expert panel, to educate the industry on new developments or concepts.

These types of shows are important to build credibility or maintain your reputation and brand awareness in the industry. In some cases, if you are not in attendance, it may indicate that your firm is not serious about the industry or not a significant enough player yet. Depending on how you participate, you can make a statement as well. If you have a large booth or are very visible, perhaps as a primary sponsor, it says, "Look at us, we are the industry leaders." Whereas a smaller presence could send a different message to the market: "We are a start-up or a new player in the industry." Both are respectable reasons for attending.

Types of Events, Trade Shows and Conferences

According to IBISWorld[8], a trusted industry research firm, "The market size, measured by revenue, of the Trade Show and Conference Planning industry was $22.4bn in 2023 (in the USA)."

Let's start by breaking it down into some bite-size pieces.

First, there are two major categories of events:

- Consumer shows (business to consumer — B2C)
  - Definition:
    - Shows that a household consumer may attend to research or purchase a product or service for their own consumption
    - E.g., home show
- Trade/industry shows (business to business — B2B)
  - Definition:
    - Shows that a buyer representing a firm may attend to research or purchase a product or service for their organization
    - E.g., HVAC supplier show

This book will focus on trade shows and conferences for business to business.

---

[8] IBIS World - https://www.ibisworld.com/

Size of Events, Trade Shows and Conferences

There are a few different sizes and types of shows and conferences. For simplicity, I have created five categories based on size, cost, location and length of event.

Micro-events (Privately Curated Events)

- Less than 100 people
- Sponsor/participant negotiation power — high — 20-50% discount
- Event length — hours to 1.5 days
- Local/regional (within driving distance)
- Non-traditional venues: museums, unique venues
- Niche
- Aliases: summit, retreat, unconference[9], non-conference, "not a conference"
- Exclusive
    - Happy hour with a program
    - Workshops
    - Sales kickoffs
    - User/peer groups / product or customer advisory group

Small

- 100-200 people
- Sponsor/participant negotiation power — high — 10-50% discount
- Event length — 0.5-2 days
- Local/regional (within driving distance)
- Hotels
- Niche
- Exclusive
    - User groups
    - Product launches
    - Awards ceremonies

---

[9] Many of these have "reduced (the) emphasis on formal speeches and instead (have) emphasized informal connections." O'Reilly, Tim (March 8, 2018). "The True Inventor of the Unconference." https://www.linkedin.com/pulse/true-inventor-unconference-tim-o-reilly/

Medium

- 201-1,500 people
- Sponsor/participant negotiation power — medium — 10-20% discount
- Event length — 1-3 days
- Regional (driving distance or short flight; 1-2 hours)
- Large hotels, small convention centers
- Horizontal- or vertical-specific
- Early business category / mature business category
  - Associations / multinational companies

Large

- 1,501-7,500 people
- Sponsor negotiation power — low — 5-10% discount
- Event length — 2-4 days
- National or international event — major city location (significant travel required)
- Large hotels, small convention centers
- Horizontal and vertical
  - Major international user group
  - Large industry event with certifications

** Pro Tip – Association Memberships Can Get You Discounts **

If you are part of an affiliated association, you may get a discount, as well as other benefits, at their primary event. Take advantage of your member benefits. Here is a sample below, Figure 2 – Membership discounts sample, demonstrating $600 off the non-member booth fees[10]. In the case below, only members get into the evening reception — an important *networking event*.

---

[10] Ontario Transportation Expo - https://ote.ca/trade-show-registration/#Member

2025 Member Trade Show Fees - OMCA, OPTA, SBO

For members of OMCA, OPTA, and SBO, registration requires your OTE-specific ID and password. For assistance, or to reserve your booth number, please contact us at info@ote.ca

Cancellation Policy: Cancellations received up to and including February 28th shall receive an 80% refund. After February 28, no refund will be available.

MEMBER	MEMBER	MEMBER
Exhibitor Booth	**Vehicle Display**	**Non-Exhibitor Access**
$1,495 /up	**$1,325** +up	**$300** /person

Exhibitor Booth
- ⚠ Subject to availability
- Includes exhibitor booth at the OTE Trade (subject to availability) and admission for up to five representatives* and two tickets to the evening reception (members only).
- Multiple booths can be purchased to create a larger booth (subject to availability).
- 🔖 PRICE: $1,495/booth

Vehicle Display
- ⚠ Subject to availability
- Vehicle Display Fees by Length of Vehicle and includes admission for up to five representatives* and two tickets to the evening reception (members only).
- 🔖 Less than 25 feet: $1,325/vehicle
- 🔖 From 25 to 40 feet: $2,100/vehicle
- 🔖 More than 40 feet: $2,400/vehicle

Non-Exhibitor Access
- ⚠ For non-exhibiting seller companies
- This is a Tuesday Day Pass for Products & Services or Business Members who do not have a booth on the trade show floor. Includes ticket to Tuesday's networking reception (reception is members only).
- 🔖 PRICE: $300/person

[Register Now] [Register Now] [Register Now]

2025 Non-Member Trade Show Fees

The following prices are for companies that are NOT current members of an OTE partner association. For membership inquiries, contact us at info@ote.ca

Cancellation Policy: Cancellations received up to and including February 28th shall receive an 80% refund. After February 28th, no refund will be available.

NON-MEMBER	NON-MEMBER	NON-MEMBER
10'x10' Booth	**Vehicle Display**	**Non-Exhibitor Access**
$2,095 /booth	**$1,925** +up	**$595**

10'x10' Booth
- ⚠ Subject to availability
- Includes exhibitor booth at the OTE Trade (subject to availability) and admission for up to five representatives.
- NOTE: Tuesday reception tickets are for members only.
- Multiple booths can be purchased to create a larger booth (subject to availability).
- 🔖 PRICE: $2,095/booth

Vehicle Display
- ⚠ Subject to availability
- Vehicle Displays are priced by Length of Vehicle and includes admission for up to five representatives.
- NOTE: Tuesday reception tickets are for members only.
- Multiple booths can be purchased to create a larger booth (subject to availability).
- 🔖 Less than 25 feet: $1,925/vehicle
- 🔖 From 25 to 40 feet: $2,700/vehicle
- 🔖 More than 40 feet: $3,000/vehicle

Non-Exhibitor Access
- ⚠ For non-exhibiting seller companies to access the OTE trade show.
- Tuesday Day Pass for Products & Services or Business Members who do not have a booth on the trade show floor.
- Includes access to Tuesday sessions and the trade show floor.
- NOTE: Tuesday reception tickets are for members only.
- 🔖 PRICE: $595/person

[Register Now] [Register Now] [Register Now]

Figure 2 – Membership discounts sample

Super Show

- 7,500+ people
- Sponsor negotiation power — low — 0-5% discount
- Event length — 3-5 days
- International event; premier industry event of the year — major city location
- Large hotels with large convention centers
- Horizontal and vertical
  - ○ Major international user group
  - ○ Multinational companies sponsoring
  - ○ Large industry event with internationally regulated certifications/licenses

Please note:

- The definitions above are generalities.
- Each vertical market may have smaller or larger numbers based on their position in the economy and compound annual growth rate expectations.
- Negotiations are always based on supply and demand and timing.

** Pro Tip – Hosting Events Within Events **

You can host a micro-event at medium to super shows as an economical way to network without the expense of buying booths or sponsoring. Some "main" events frown upon this practice because they perceive you as competition or a "cheap" workaround, while others embrace your idea as they see you as an enhancement or another reason for people to attend the central event. It's all about return on investment for all participants (show owner, vendors, attendees).

Chapter 2 – Return on Event (ROE)

Event and Trade Show math has been an age-old philosophical and financial discussion going back centuries to the original fairs and markets. The bottom line has always been the bottom line. Opportunity costs are always a consideration. Patience and purpose are also longer term items that factor into decisions.

Today, we're in an era of data-driven decision-making, so in this section we are trading guesswork for quantifiable theories and fiscal responsibility.

Events are not cheap in the 21st century, so it is critical to maximize the return on investment (ROI) or to establish the payback period, or time to first deal, for you and your firm. I like to think of all of these as a Return on Event (ROE). Whatever you call it, alignment is critical between the Finance team or the budget holder(s) and the Marketing and Sales teams.

It should be noted that in many cases, ROI is confused with the Payback Period. To disambiguate, the difference between the two is discussed below. If you are not a finance or math person, don't worry; worksheets are provided in Appendix B and C.

This **QR Code** can be used to access online worksheets at paulabdool.ca.

Return on Investment (ROI) Formula

Return (R) = [Final Value (Vf) – Initial Value (Vi)] / [Initial Value (Vi) x 100]

- R = return
- Vf = final value (i.e., revenue earned attributed to the event)
- Vi = initial value

ROI is an estimate of an investment's profitability. ROI is calculated by subtracting the initial cost (or value) of the investment from its final cost (or value), then dividing this new number by the cost of the investment, then multiplying it by 100 to get a percentage.

The ROI of an event should be in line with the ROI of other marketing activities.

See Appendix B – Return on Investment Worksheet.

Payback Period (PP) Formula

Payback Period = Initial Investment / Annual Cash Inflows

The payback period is calculated by dividing the initial investment by the annual cash inflows. The initial investment is the cost involved in the event, and annual cash inflows is the cash your company expects to receive from the investment in a designated period or annually. This of course depends on the length of your sales cycles.

In my opinion, the PP methodology is better than the ROI on an event-by-event basis. The ROI is a better overall view of your annual event budget.

See Appendix C – Payback Period Worksheet

Time to First Deal

This is simple. Time to first deal is from the time you get home from the event to the time it takes to get your first deal or signed contract. It is the sibling of the payback period, but it can be very skewed for multiple reasons. It could be weeks or months, or a deal might not come for a year or two, depending on buying cycles, current contract terms with competitors, RFP processes or other macroeconomic events or hurdles.

As a rule, the time to first deal should provide a breakeven for the event within an agreed-upon period.

Timing examples based on average sale cycle lengths:

- First deal (transactional) = less than 2 months
- First deal (mid-market / small medium business [SMB]) = 3-6 months
- First deal (enterprise) = 7-12 months

If your firm conducts all of the above business transaction types, then you may factor all of those into the ROI, payback period and time to first deal metrics.

Trade Show Math – The Financial Caveats

Let's get something absolutely straight! Trade show math is a crazy calculus-like equation.

You do not always get an immediate payback or a return on your event. It could take weeks to get a follow-up meeting or to book and get demos completed. It could take two times the length of your average sales cycle to see your first deal because of scheduling conflicts and conference seasonality. Depending on where you are in your fiscal year, the return could happen in the next fiscal year (e.g., October event and your fiscal year ends in December).

It is critical to establish the ROE (ROI and/or payback period) before you start to ensure that the people who are watching the bottom line and will write the check for the next event are in full agreement about what success looks like.

Although ROI, payback periods and time to first deals are very important key success factors, they all mess with traditional academic math. Accounting is very black-and-white, and trade show math is gray and skewed by philosophies.

For example, if you get a $1,000,000 deal after participating in an event that cost $100,000, should you go next year, or should you take your ROI and invest it somewhere else? Should you spend $200,000 next year, betting on the "fact" that you will get two $1,000,000 deals? If in year 2, you do not get a deal, was the year 2 investment already covered by the initial $1,000,000 deal?

These are all discussions you should have in order to manage expectations and establish budgets for the next season or determine if you will be able to invest in this type of marketing in the future.

You should also consider comparing the overall event costs to other marketing customer acquisition costs (CAC). If the CAC is similar to or better than other go-to-market activities, it may be an area that you double down on. If it is more costly, then you might consider just attending key events or participating as an attendee to remain "close to the street" — or not attending at all.

It is important that you think of events as affecting the entire funnel. However, I suggest that you consider two types of macro funnels or models to really maximize your return on event.

1. Marketing funnel
2. Bowtie — mirrored funnel

Marketing Funnel

Traditionally, marketers have used the top of funnel (TOFU), middle of funnel (MOFU) and bottom of funnel (BOFU) models to conduct their activities and to measure success. These apply to events and the activities before and after the events. For simplicity, the three stages can be summarized as follows:

- TOFU, three months before: Build awareness, generate interest, and drive booth traffic.
- MOFU, during the show: Engage, educate, and qualify prospects for deeper conversations.
- BOFU, three months after: Convert leads, measure impact, and nurture long-term relationships.

Top of Funnel (TOFU) – Three Months Before the Show

Goal: Build awareness and generate interest in your brand before the event.

Key activities:

- Target audience identification — Define ideal prospects and key decision-makers.
- Pre-show marketing — Launch email campaigns, LinkedIn ads, and blog content to create buzz.
- Social media announcements — Promote the event with teasers, countdowns and speaker highlights.
- Lead magnet development — Create valuable pre-show content like e-books, guides or exclusive webinars.
- Booth and demo prep — Develop engaging booth materials, signage and interactive demos.
- Outreach to attendees — Use event apps, email and social media to schedule meetings before the show.

Middle of Funnel (MOFU) – During the Show

Goal: Engage and nurture prospects by building relationships and gathering qualified leads.

Key activities:

- Live booth engagement — Deliver compelling product demos and host Q and A sessions.
- Lead capture and qualification — Use digital tools such as scanners and Customer Relationship Management (CRM) integrations to track visitor interactions.

- Networking and meetings — Attend private events, one-on-one meetings, and panel discussions.
- Content distribution — Provide brochures, case studies and promo items to educate potential buyers.
- Live social media updates — Share real-time event highlights, customer testimonials and behind-the-scenes content.
- Exclusive show offers — Offer limited-time discounts or incentives to encourage immediate interest.

Bottom of Funnel (BOFU) – Three Months After the Show

Goal: Convert trade show leads into customers, and measure ROI.

Key activities:

- Follow-up campaigns — Send personalized emails and LinkedIn messages to re-engage booth visitors.
- Lead scoring and prioritization — Categorize leads based on interest level and readiness to buy.
- Sales outreach and demos — Schedule follow-up calls and product demos for highly engaged prospects.
- Retargeting ads — Run targeted ads to reinforce messaging to attendees who interacted with your brand.
- Webinars and case studies — Share success stories and deeper insights to nurture warm leads.
- Performance analysis — Evaluate event ROI by tracking deals closed, pipeline growth, and engagement metrics.

For more information on the marketing funnel, check out Karen Taylor's blog post, "The Digital Marketing Funnel is Evolving. Are You Prepared?"[11] She discusses and agrees with the scientific bowtie model that describes the integration of the early funnel stages and profitable sales growth.

---

[11] https://www.kunocreative.com/blog/digital-marketing-funnel-evolving

Bowtie – Mirrored Funnel

In the case of software-as-a-service (SaaS) or any other potential recurring revenue services, event math can be further complicated. Attribution may be looked at from a variety of angles — see Figure 3 – Go-to-market motions mapped to the Winning by Design bowtie model. In the customer acquisition phase or traditional selling zone, you may not get a new deal or logo right away. However, in the customer retention or expansion phase, you may hold on to a customer that was considering a competitor, or they may even buy other products from you — expansion. Both prospective customers and current customers should be considered in the trade show equation.

Acquisition Phase	Retention and Expansion Phase
Awareness	Retention
Education	Expansion
New sales	

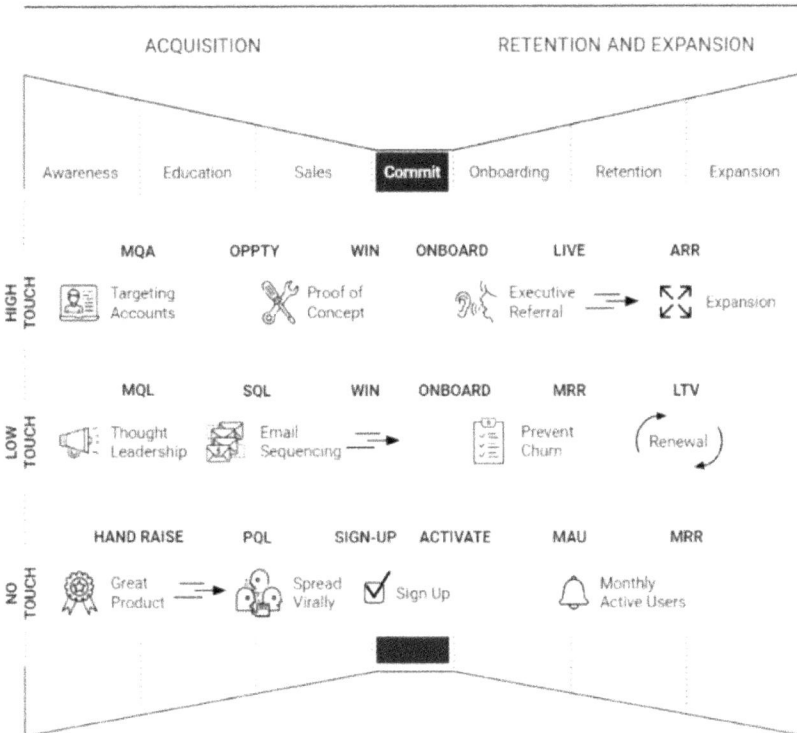

Figure 3 – Go-to-market motions mapped to the Winning by Design bowtie model[12]

---

[12] https://winningbydesign.com/

> "If I could go back in time 10 years and give myself life-altering advice, it would be this:
>
> - Getting to conferences is game-changing.
> - Build business communities in real life, whenever and wherever possible.
> - Building these communities outside your organization is a must!"
>
> Monique Moran
> CEO, Growth Assembly

Success could, and in my opinion should, be measured by any or all of the following.

Attribution (aka who gets the credit for bringing in the business)

One of many prospect touchpoints and part of an overall attribution model.

- Examples:
    - Eight of your prospects are attending, three of them are making a decision by the end of the year, and one or two of them buy your product or service within six months of the show.
    - Five of your customers are in attendance, they are due to renew their contracts next year, and Customer Success has been unable to reach them.
    - Twelve new prospects are met and are added to your nurture list.
    - Two thousand attendees now know the name of your company and what you do.

Partners

- Examples:
    - New partners are added to your network.
    - They introduce you to five new prospects within six months of the event.
    - You do a combined demo and value proposition meeting at the event.

26

Competitive intelligence

- Example:
    - You are short-listed for a deal, and it is between you and a competitor that was at the show. You learn that their average contract value is three times as much as yours and some current customers are not happy with a certain feature that was promised. You exploit this knowledge to win that deal.

References and insights

- Example:
    - One of your customers provides insights to how things are going since they acquired your product and agrees to be a reference for you on a current deal.

Case studies

- Example:
    - You present a case study at the show with a customer, and you get three new prospects.

News and announcements

- Examples:
    - Maybe your firm acquired another firm, or you were acquired. You describe it in person to the market in a very public forum by participating as a speaker or sponsoring an opening keynote speaker.
    - Maybe you want to announce a new solution or partnership that has a short competitive advantage lifespan.
        - You may have a head start on the market because you have solved a problem that the market must deal with, like a regulation change or a new law. This may be your window to exploit it before fast followers catch up.

"Show Me the Money"

There is nothing better than to "put cash" in Finance's hands and for you or your manager to shout that from the attribution hill. This is where the gray of non-transactional collides with the black and white of transactional. On the business side, you need to make money. Finance's patience and timelines are shorter. On the personal side, you need to make deposits in the social capital account. The balance is important.

- Examples:
    - The show costs $30,000 to participate in, and you get a $30,000 client within six months of the show
    - You can directly attribute a first touch attribution to the show
        - Meeting #1
        - Demo #1
        - A full sales cycle
        - A contract
    - ROI = 100%[13]
    - Payback period = six months
    - Time to first deal = six months

Some other reasons that people go to the marquee events:

- "Club" and branding
    - Your company and you need to be "like water on the shore" … you keep rolling in and you become part of the fabric, community or "club." These public appearances solidify your brand.
- Create your board of trusted advisors
    - Throughout the year or between events, you will need answers or support. You may not have all the answers, but you want to know who does.
- Fun with friends and colleagues
    - After attending events for a while, they can become more fun because you get to know more people.

---

[13] It should be noted that the revenue is the ROE, because it covers the CAC, but the profit levels will be based on the firm's pricing and profit model. For example, net profit might be 35%.

Establishing an Annual Event Budget

In October, or two months before the end of your fiscal year, a show or event budget should be established. This can be done in a few ways. If you are starting from scratch, you should understand the overall marketing budget for the organization. Trade shows and event marketing are part of the marketing mix. For easy math, if your firm's marketing budget was a million dollars, the trade show or event marketing budget may carve out a portion of the million dollars, or it may be additive if events are new to the firm. Marketing is an investment, so getting a return on that event must be carefully considered when determining the budget. To do this you have to start by knowing your costs — see Appendix D – Annual Event Budget Template and Planner.

Establishing an Event Budget

The event / trade show math information above could inform your budget, or events could become a strategic investment based on a change in your business or the industry you belong to.

Regardless of your firm's philosophy or reasons to participate, establishing a budget is a good business practice. It contains spending and informs all parties of what they can and cannot do from a financial perspective. Each event must have its own stand-alone budget that rolls up to the master annual event and marketing or departmental budget. These budgets need to include:

- Fees to participate in the event
- Sponsorships
- Entertainment
    - Meals for clients or prospective clients
    - Bar budgets
- Travel for all involved
    - Flights
    - Taxis/ride shares
    - Meals
    - Hotels

** Pro Tip – The Hotel Choice **

- Stay at the main hotel or one of the other recommended hotels close to the venue, even if it costs a little more. Why?
- Two "stumble factors"
    - You have a higher percentage opportunity to run into show attendees in the elevator, halls, gyms, restaurants, check-in/check-out, bathrooms, coffee shops, and outdoor areas.

- o Being an elevator ride away from your room allows you to accomplish the following:
  - Reduce ride share/taxi costs
  - Maximize the Workout to Last Call networking opportunities
  - Share shuttles to and from events that are "off campus" or to the airport
  - Allow for rest time between events (e.g., short nap or time to call home)
  - Change efficiently into appropriate attire for evening events
  - Go to your room for a must-attend meeting
- Booths/ Stands
  - o Booth setup and takedown fees
    - If you set it up with your staff, it is "free."
      - However, many large shows and certain convention centers and hotels are unionized and may have a drayage[14] rule/policy — this can become expensive.
  - o Booth decorating and tools/tech
    - Booth decorating and maintenance: Pop-up stands, signage, carpet, electricity, monitors, lighting, furniture, garbage cans
    - Shipping costs (drayage)
    - Giveaways
    - Badge scanners
  - o People — brand ambassadors
    - Opportunity costs
    - Team shirts or outfits

See Appendix E – Event Budget Worksheet.

---

[14] In trade shows, drayage refers to the transportation of exhibit materials from a shipping dock or warehouse to a booth space within a convention center, and back after the event. It includes unloading, storing empty crates, and reloading after the show.

Attendee Business Case

Your firm may or may not be attending the event. If they are attending the event, they may have criteria for individuals to attend[15]. If you believe that you should attend the event, you may have to also build and provide a business case. I discuss a variety of ways to justify your attendance at an event below.

Training, Education, Continuing Education

Training is probably the best and most common way to cost justify attendance at a professional event. To do our day-to-day jobs, we need to be up-to-date about the industry that we participate in daily. If we are not aware of happenings, or of sentiments from customers/partners, industry pundits, analysts and futurists, we will fall behind. In many companies, there are professional development funds that often go unused. Use them: they are for your development, and they will make you a better employee.

Certification

A part of training is certification. Many industries and associations have certifications that keep your skills sharp or might be critical to your advancement in your profession. Participating in those events or in-person classes may be the only way to gain or maintain continuing education credits or professional certification units (PCUs) for certain certifications. Professional development funds may also be used for these.

Market Knowledge

In my opinion, this may be one of the most important overall elements about participating in industry events. It is hard to quantify or measure but should always be part of the conversation. Many events hold seminars and workshops providing significant takeaways that can change how you work.

This information can sometimes be gleaned from reading a book or taking online courses. However, people learn in different ways, and some of the best speakers, with the best research and experience, are the leaders of these workshops. You may also benefit from their participation in expert panels and from interaction with the audience. You may hear pros and cons that they cannot document in a journal. You may also be able to ask your questions directly to them in an "offline" manner at a mixer or another informal time. They may invite you to add them to your "I know a person" network that has answers to questions you have not even thought of yet.

---

[15] For example, an account executive can attend if three or more prospects are attending, or an account manager can attend if three or more current customers are attending; or marketing can go if the show has more than 250 attendees.

These industry pundits stay more current than you because it is their job, and if you know them, you may have access to the answers. It could be the difference between winning and losing a deal.

The Scout

You may be the buyer or leader of a buying committee. You may have been tasked with researching a new product or system. These events are a live marketplace for your research. A place to not only hear from the vendors but also their customers and others that may have worked with them in the past. You may learn about pricing models or ways to save money that you cannot figure out from online research.

If you are lucky, there may be a head-to-head discussion or a panel discussion, to help provide clarity during your evaluation. You also may get access to people that you would not normally speak to during your evaluation.

Networking

On the other side, you might be trying to get in front of decision-makers and their buying committee. They may be there evaluating and asking questions. You may be able to meet with them and get to know answers or the reasons they might buy. You also may be able to meet with them in informal places and learn more about them.

You may be able to earn their trust.

Let me say that again: you might earn their trust.

Nobody buys anything if they don't trust you!

From an efficiency standpoint, decision-makers with whom it would take you months to book meetings, or to travel to their individual companies to meet with them and/or their colleagues, may all be in one place. You may also be able to learn about the dynamics of their relationships. For example, who is on your side, who is a detractor or hanging out with your competitor, or who actually has the political capital or "juice" in their organization. All of these interactions can be the difference between winning and losing. Do you want the relationship and knowledge advantage, or will your competitors gain it and use it to beat you?

You may also be able to meet with several customers or prospective customers all within a few days, which will save you money and time. You may potentially be able to get current customers to be a live reference for you and to demonstrate that others trust you!

See Appendix A — Email Template to Manager and Attendee Business Case.

Chapter 3 – The Organizer's Chapter

Congrats! You have put your hand up to take on a major activity. This can be a full-time job or part of your role as a marketer.

What will you be doing behind-the-scenes and in front of the world?

Here is a sample job description:

- Oversee scheduling, registration and logistics for B2B events, conferences and trade shows.
- Manage program execution, ensuring all event details are completed on time.
- Facilitate seamless coordination between internal teams and external partners.
- Collaborate with Marketing, Demand Generation, and Product teams on messaging and pre-event campaigns.
- Work with vendors on booth design, and coordinate logistics with show management.
- Travel to events and ensure the company's success on-site.
- Be the main point of contact for all event-related activities, ensuring the team is aligned and prepared.

> "Tomorrow is often the busiest day
> of the week."
>
> Old Spanish Proverb

The point of the proverb above is to do what you can before the event. Accomplish the "to-do list" items that you can before the heat of the event rises, so you do not cut corners as the pressure increases.

As an organizer, you want everything to be perfect. This is a great starting place, but please allow yourself the grace to be imperfect. Events unfold imperfectly in the real world. So, shoot for 100%, and be satisfied with less than perfect.

Why?

Because you are the only person that knows what 100% looks like. You have set the bar for you. So, if you fall short in your own mind, it probably looks perfect to others. Even if it is 100% in your mind, the critics will come out of the woodwork and provide unsolicited feedback about how it could have been better. Listen to the feedback, digest it and raise the bar for next time. You will never, ever, satisfy everyone.

With all this said, your road to a "perfect" event starts with good planning, checklists and being organized.

Be proactive and steady.

Let's get started.

Marketing

This whole book is about marketing at an event ... either your company or you or both!

If nobody knows who you are, what you do, why you do it and the value that you provide to them, you will not make money, and you will not progress on your mission or in your career.

To accomplish spreading the news about your company or you, you must get out on the street where the decision-makers, analysts, partners and competitors are.

You need to show up!

You don't have to be perfect, but you must work hard at spreading the message. Your message may even evolve during the event or after the event. You will learn more about the market and where you fit in it. You will learn what is missing in the market, or the event may expose your weaknesses to work on.

Show up!

It is easier said than done, so the following section will describe some tactical steps to take before, during and after the event.

Pre-event – T-minus Three Months

During the weeks leading up to the event, your marketing plan must crescendo up to the event start date. All your plans should be rock solid a minimum of four to eight weeks[16] out and be ready to execute methodically, like planes arriving on the runway.

Here are some tactical items to consider completing.

Messaging and the Team

Prior to the event, you must plan the message that you want to share early. Preferably months before the event. Your message needs to be like water on the shore, consistent and persistent. Above all, it needs to be simple!

> "If you can't explain it simply, you don't understand it well enough."
>
> Albert Einstein

Each department involved in presales or customer retention needs to be aware of your plan to participate in the event. These departments include Marketing and Sales (of course), Product, Customer Success, Partner Channel leaders and managers, and Finance.

Yes, Finance. They are the ones that will support or decline future investments, so involving them and showing that you respect and appreciate the profit and loss (P and L) component of events will go a long way. Believe me, when you submit your expenses, they will start the clock on looking for an ROE or some payback.

Naturally, Sales, Marketing and Product should be closer to the actual "street" and should provide or even lead messaging. This needs to be very consistent leading up to the show and supported by blogs and lead-up events, like webinars, podcasts, videos and other content.

The messaging should inform all of the content. It could be the basis of your booth design, brand ambassador shirts, giveaways and demos.

---

[16] This could vary depending on the size and complexity of the setup and the number of variables involved.

The attendees are inundated with messages when they walk down the aisles. Make your booth more like a billboard than a brochure.

"Pause for a moment and think, 'If I replaced the logo on this booth with someone else's, would it still work?'

If yes, come up with a new idea, otherwise you're going to fade into the depths of forgettableness."

Mac Reddin
CEO, Commsor

High-level Messaging Components

- Unique value proposition (UVP or Value Prop) or tagline
    - Your value prop or tagline should clearly describe the value of your product or services
    - Examples:
        - Uber — The Smartest Way to Get Around
        - Apple iPhone — The Experience IS the Product
        - Slack — Be More Productive at Work with Less Effort
- Distinctive value
    - The key ideas that you want prospects to learn regarding what is unique about your product or services
    - Examples:
        - Patented super widget
        - Only domestically produced products
        - 100% woman-owned business
        - Gluten-free
- Evidence
    - Differentiators that demonstrate your distinctive value
    - Examples:
        - Since 1960
        - Award-winning
        - Used in over 40 countries
        - 90% of dentists recommend us
- Personas
    - Who should do business with you
    - Examples:
        - C-suite
        - Developers
        - Marketers
        - Accountants
- Use cases
    - Why other customers have bought your product to eliminate their pain or to fulfill their requirements
    - Examples:
        - To satisfy regulatory requirements for government ABC
        - To reduce time to market
        - To reduce the amount of people that abandon a cart at checkout
        - To lower their cholesterol

Event Schedule Sharing on Social Media

How many times do you see someone only post about their event on LinkedIn or other social media when they are at the airport or standing in their fully set-up booth? Although these are good reminders for people that are tracking a hashtag or an event, these messages are only reminders.

What should you do?

Here is a great example of sharing your personal event schedule or your company's schedule in advance. In this example, you will see that the CMO shared her schedule for the quarter well in advance.

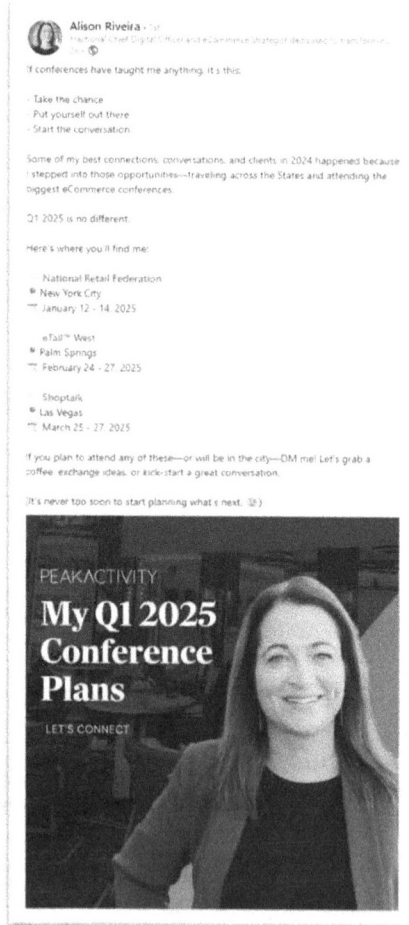

Figure 4 – Pre-conference meeting schedule sample

Why is this advance notice important?

It becomes part of an overall marketing plan to socialize actively with your followers and prospective customers at events, and it provides a gentle signal that you would like to meet with them. It may also provide your Marketing and Sales team with a great jumping-off point to begin to book meetings.

If you read the fine print in the post above, you will notice in the parenthesis that Alison said, "It's never too soon to start planning what's next."

Show Templates for Social Media

If you contract to be a sponsor or for a booth, the show owner's Marketing team may provide you with some templates to further proliferate news about the show. These templates can provide easy ways to create a quick social media post by inserting your company logo and your website or even attendees to contact.

This is a symbiotic relationship between the sponsor and the show management team because they can also provide a discount from your post to encourage more attendees to participate. If they provide a customer QR code for you, there might be some bonuses for you, like tickets to a VIP event.

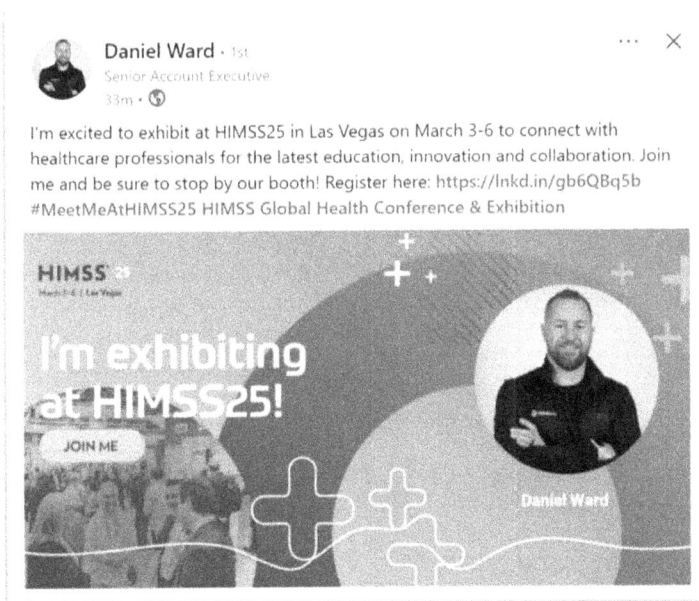

Figure 5 – Sample pre-show template

Video and Photography Preparation

Videos and pictures are an absolute must in today's world of marketing and social media. You do not need a lot of equipment or to spend a lot of money (see Video Tech Stack options/levels below). What you do need is to carve out time to take photos and footage before, during and after the event. When things get busy, this is an area that can go astray. You cannot take too many pictures or videos.

** Pro Tip – Video Tech Stack **

I experienced pre- and post-event vlogs[17] by my friend Emma Lo[18], and they always created a buzz and FOMO (fear of missing out). She shared a few tech stack tips with me.

Level 1

1. Smartphone — you already have one
2. Social media account
   a. LinkedIn, Instagram, TikTok, Facebook, X
   b. A company account is best, but you can post to a personal account for your own personal branding. Business plans are available.

Level 2

Includes Level 1 plus the following components:

1. Video editor app — free to $50 USD / month
   a. Here are a few available brands: CapCut, VEED, Node Video, or Clipchamp
   b. There are some free versions, but I suggest that you subscribe to get the features that will help you make better quality videos (e.g., adding music, better editing features, etc.).
2. Lavalier microphone (cool kids call it a lav mic or a lapel mic) — $75-$200 USD
   a. They are Bluetooth ready and can be accessed by a smartphone or an economical video camera.
   b. These can be held by someone that you are interviewing, or they can be clipped to your shirt as you are shooting your videos.

---

[17] Vlogs: Video logs
[18] https://www.linkedin.com/in/emma-lo/

Figure 6 – Sample lav mics (OSA and Hollyland)

Level 3

Includes Level 2 plus the following components:

1. Video editor app for interview editing — $15 - $40 USD / month
   a. Here are a few brands: OpusClip, Simplified, Synthesia or Prezi.
   b. These take your editing up a notch to create good evergreen content.
2. DSLR camera — $500-$2,500 USD
   a. Here are a few brands: Sony, Canon, Nikon
   b. These are fantastic for capturing quality photos and videos for vlogging and social media posts. Also great for doing live posts from an event.
3. Lighting
   a. Ring light — $40-$200 USD

Figure 7 – Sample ring light with tripod and remote

4. Special apparatus — some or all the items below are available in packages
    a. Selfie sticks — $15-$100 USD
    b. Tripods — $50-$700 USD
    c. Camera stabilizers — $100-$400 USD
        i. Gimbal[19]
            • According to a blog[20] by Alec Chillingworth, a content writer at Epidemic Sound, "The gimbal senses the difference between your intentional movements and small, unwanted interruptions like shakiness." He suggests that "Using a gimbal cuts out the need for a dedicated camera operator while still delivering stable, high-quality footage."

Figure 8 – Tripod, selfie stick, gimbal and remote control

---

[19] A gimbal is a pivoted support that allows for the rotation of an object about an axis. Most gimbals will either be two-axis or three-axis. Source: https://nofilmschool.com/what-is-a-gimbal-definition
[20] https://www.epidemicsound.com/blog/what-is-a-gimbal-and-how-to-use-one/

Speaker's Tech Stack

Speaking at an event can be very beneficial. The opportunity could:

1. Showcase your expertise
2. Position your company in the market
3. Provide an overview and demonstration of your product to drive traffic to your booth or to book meetings

Regardless of your motivations, your tech better work as hard as you.

The speaker tech stack is underrated!

You work hard on your presentation, you practice ... maybe you have some butterflies ... and then the audiovisual (AV) setup is lacking what you need.

There is nothing worse than showing up to present and they have not done a great job setting you up for success. Your computer isn't compatible with the projector cords, the sound isn't working, and they don't have a slide advancer (i.e., clicker) in the room.

Most quality conferences will have a universal "speaker room" for you to test all of this beforehand, or they may even have you send your presentation ahead of time so it can be preloaded on the laptop in the room you are presenting.

BUT ... if you are on the conference circuit enough, I highly recommend that you bring your own tool kit. See Figure 9 – Speaker's tool kit.

1. Clicker/slide advancer — $20-$50 USD
2. Dongle or adapter to get the HDMI plug into your computer — $30-$100 USD
3. Speaker — if you have sound or are playing a video in your presentation — $100-$400 USD
4. If you have a critical takeaway or a summary of your presentation, print out a few copies.

Figure 9 – Speaker's tool kit

Booth/Stand Location

Once you decide that you will be attending a show, the position of your booth is critical to your success to ensure high traffic. Choosing your position early is important because prime and preferred positions will go fast. For example, near entrances, on data-driven footpaths, near food and beverage stations, or near or far from competitors.

Entrances

Being near the entrance to the show is good because everyone needs to pass your booth to see what is inside; however, they may do a "drive-by" if they are drawn to something further in. For example, Booth 128 or 132 in Figure 10 below may be a drive-by booth upon entrance. If you can be near the entrance that is closest to the meeting rooms or the direction of the flow of people (i.e., near keynote stages or ballrooms, large lunchrooms or escalators leading to the show floor) this can ensure that you are seen.

Locating your booth in the area where people are more likely to start gives you a huge competitive advantage over the other booths in the trade show. Remember, you don't want to be on the other end of the exhibition hall, such as Booth 113, because the longer the attendees are on the trade show floor, the less engaged they become.

Left Side or Right Side of the Exhibition Hall?

According to Selby's[21], an event display company, "studies have shown that trade show attendees in countries where the driver is on the left, start on the right side of the exhibition hall. On the other hand, countries with drivers on the right are more likely to start from the left." So, in North America pick the right side of a trade show floor, relative to the entrance. See Figure 10 – Sample trade show layout.

---

[21] Source: Custom Flags, Banners, Exhibition Stands and Signage by Selby's

Follow the data and put your booth on the footpath.

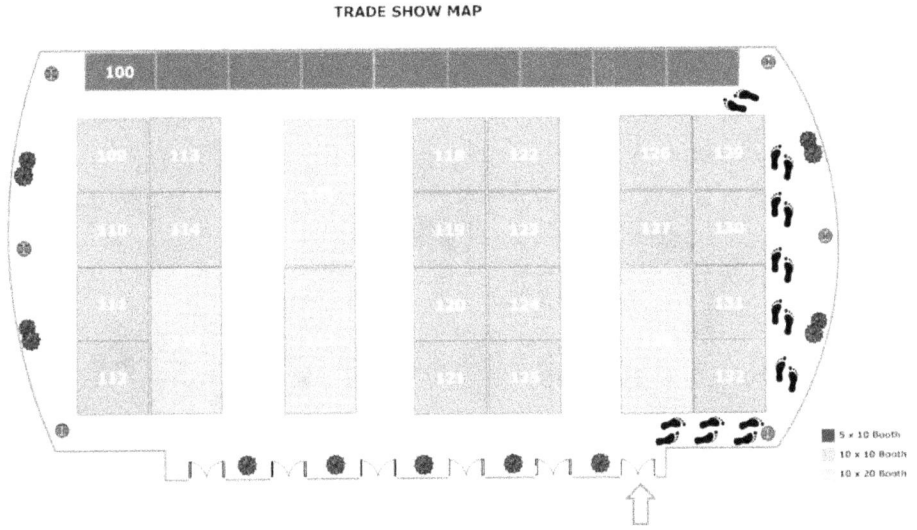

Figure 10 – Sample trade show layout

Food and Beverage Stations

Being near food and beverage stations are great as well because almost everyone will pass by your booth or near to it. It is also a good place to direct people to your booth while they are sipping on their pick-me-up beverage or nibbling their energizing snack. If you have a table or even a place to sit, it allows you to offer a brief resting place while you discuss your product over a coffee. This is a utopian state. However, you must work to get them in there. More on that later in Chapter 4 – At the Event.

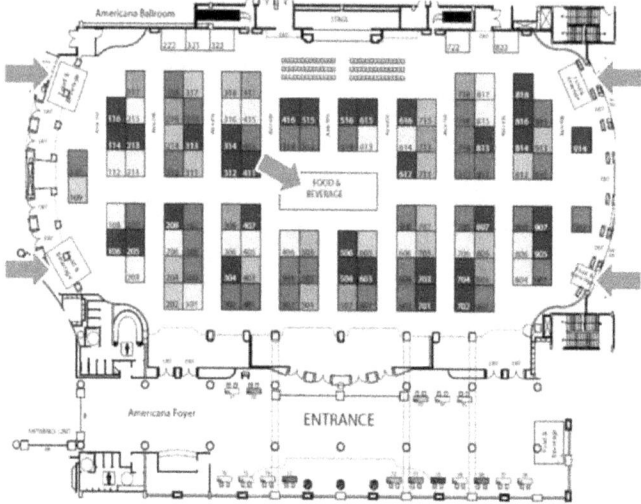

Figure 11 – Proximity to food and beverage stations

Near Partners – Synergies

Locating near partners to encourage symbiotic conversations and easy pass-offs to each other can be invaluable. This may extend conversations and allow you to gain more information about problems, buying committees, past experiences, relationships or other nuances that will help you gain the business in the future.

An underutilized benefit or byproduct is the buzz that you can create between your booths. It can create an energetic and boisterous environment that can attract more people. It can also allow you to team up with each other to encourage others to visit your respective booths.

You could split a booth like Booth 117 or get Booths 123 and 127. See Figure 12 – Partner or competition booth positioning.

** Pro Tip – Booth Gift Synergy **

An example of synergy or booth attraction: Attendees may get half of their gift in one booth and the second part in the other. The gift or giveaway is incomplete if they don't stop at both booths. A sample — a cup and a coaster, or a remote control and a car.

Near Competitors – Direct Comparisons

This is a bold move, but sometimes it makes sense to be near your competition, such as Booths 123 and 127. It allows you to hear their messaging, see who they are talking with and catch some apples falling off their metaphorical tree.

In busy times, they can't talk to everyone at once, so you may get some spillover traffic.

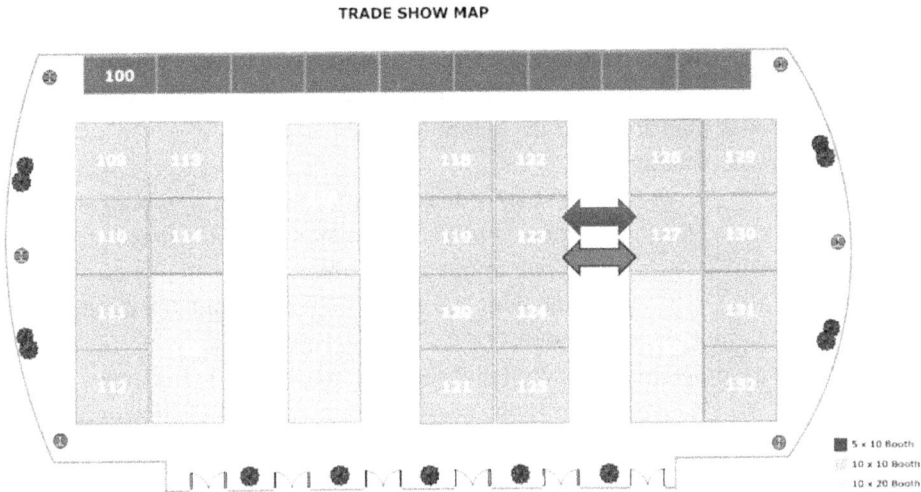

Figure 12 – Partner or competition booth positioning

Their prospects or customers may boldly ask you, "How are you different and/or better?", which will give you the opportunity to outshine your competitor in a head-to-head battle.

Please note:

The ball bounces both ways and you must be confident about your booth, your product and your brand ambassadors. It could backfire too if your competitor outworks, outsmarts or simply is better than you.

** Pro Tip – Use Lead Retrieval Applications **

Scanning badges has evolved to using apps that are licensed to companies by the user. I highly recommend arming at least one person at the booth with the ability to scan badges (e.g., SmartSource)[22]. This is critical for efficiency during busy times.

- Do scan multiple people from the same company.
  - If people are traveling together to an event, this can demonstrate a buying intention (i.e., budget established or budget being established, research from a variety of angles by a buying committee).
  - The scans could be critical for later in the buying cycle or customer journey. These people could all impact the decision-making process, and their personas should be captured for multi-threading opportunities during the sales process.
  - Note: These people should be appropriately approached by your team during networking events. If a dinner is held, then the seating plan should be by persona.
  - Cautions:
    - More scans does not equal more opportunities.
    - This can be a misleading statistic that can lead to disappointment or bad trade show math, when it comes to evaluating the value of the event and the quality of attendees.
- Do preprogram information that you want to gather into the apps.
  - Most apps today can capture one to ten qualification or discovery questions, and you can also add notes in a free-form section.
  - Many of the apps allow you to rate the prospect with a 1-3 rating (hot, warm, cool) to focus post-show follow-ups and meeting scheduling.
- Do work as a team when talking to a prospect if possible.
  - One person should scan and enter information while the other person talks to the prospect.

---

[22] https://thesmartsource.com/event-management-solutions/lead-retrieval/

- The person entering information into the application should be actively involved in the conversation to ensure that no questions are missed.
- There may also be a free-form area to enter other items that come up.

Within the portal, you can:
- Add custom questions / company-specific qualifiers
- Offer personalized surveys
- Send follow-up emails with marketing and sales materials
- Access reporting tools
- Download leads post-show

Here are some sample questions to enter into the lead retrieval application. These preprogrammed questions can ensure that you are thorough in your high-level discovery and qualification of prospects. In addition, preprogramming keeps questions consistent. It also allows you to segment and measure the leads by quality level after the show.

- What is your current role, and what responsibilities does it entail?
- What specific challenges are you hoping to address through solutions at this event?
- How familiar are you with our industry, and have you used similar products/services before?
- What aspects of your business are you looking to improve in the next six months?
- On a scale of 1 to 10, how interested are you in exploring new solutions?
- Are there any particular features or functionalities you prioritize when evaluating products?
- Are you willing to share your preferred mode of communication for post-event follow-up?
- There are usually some free-form areas to enter other items that come up.

Sponsoring or Exhibiting

Strategies to drive traffic to your booth or event are critical to maximizing your investment. As a sponsor, you should get a fair number of tools and support from the show company itself, things like collateral or easy-to-market tools and graphics that you can leverage in your own social media marketing or other channels that you decide to use.

Booth Design

Having a booth is useless if nobody talks to you or you don't attract them to your message. Some ideas to attract prospective customers to you are below:

- Bright colors and lights — your brand ambassador outfits, or your booth design, really help.
- Simple messaging — your pre-event messaging or tagline should make it easy to understand your offering but be vague enough to make someone curious to engage in conversation (e.g., "We make you money while you sleep").
- Coffee station with barista — who doesn't want a free custom beverage or a quality pick-me-up at an event where the beverage offerings are not always the best? More importantly, it provides between 60 seconds and 2 minutes to get your message across, scan badges and qualify leads.
- Book giveaways — if you have an industry expert or someone that has participated in a seminar with you that has written a book, it can be a fantastic draw to your booth. While the author is autographing copies, you can be qualifying leads or scanning badges.
- Movement — balls, putting greens, or a spinning wheel of giveaways can be a little tacky, but they often garner a lot of attention and can bring out the competitive nature of small buying committees. These are economical and draw the eye to the booth. Don't let them be the only thing you focus on. All these things need to be on message and allow you to quickly express your value to the prospects.
- Massages — these are great on day 2 or 3 of a long event and can get a prospect talking during the massage or while they wait their turn. This is not a high-turn tool but can work if you have a demo that takes more than five minutes to show.
- Comfortable couches — your prospects' feet are tired from walking around an event. If you have the room or have a demonstration at your booth, comfortable chairs will keep prospects there longer.
- Private happy hour or an "unauthorized event within the event"
  - By buying the minimum package governed by the show, you are complying. Then you can bring your own stuff to top up what they

provide. You can even reserve the "good stuff" for special prospects or customers.

- o This can also be done outside of the main host hotel bar. You can invite people from the show to this event. This will reduce their expenses, and it will allow you to have some longer conversations while drinks are prepared.
- Tchotchkes
  - o Definition[23]: a small, cheap, ornamental trinket or souvenir; a knickknack
  - o Usually branded with company logos
    - Samples below in Figure 13 – Tchotchkes and giveaways (e.g., socks, pens, coasters, magnets, mini-speakers, phone chargers, eyeglass cleaners, gum, mints, notebooks, bookmarks)
  - o Alternative spellings: chotchke, tchachke, chachki

Figure 13 – Tchotchkes and giveaways

---

[23] https://www.dictionary.com/browse/tchotchke

- A significant giveaway
  - If you have the means to provide a substantial giveaway (i.e., greater than $200 in value), people will enter their names in the draw. This can be both good and bad.
    - Good is if you have a conversation with someone and there is a small but not tedious barrier to entry, like watching a brief demo.
    - Bad is if you just have a bowl collecting business cards or forms that are easy to fill out.
    - You can also have a two-tiered giveaway of a semi-valuable item for the business card droppers and a more valuable item for the people that spend time with you.
- Puppies — yes, puppies
  - Shelters will often partner with booths to allow a few puppies to hang out in your booth, if you donate to the shelter or try to place the puppies with new homes.
  - They will provide you with dog handlers; don't worry, you won't have to clean up, all you have to do is snuggle and talk to customers.

Figure 14 – Puppies within a pen near the company's booth

Pre-event – T-minus Four Weeks

Getting the Message Out

- Social media
    - Social media is an economical and straightforward way to execute pre-event messaging.
    - Shows now provide art and quick links to begin the advertising campaigns. This can be as simple as "we will be there" messaging, especially if you are a sponsor or exhibiting.
    - However, creating a campaign that is multifaceted can be richer and more memorable.

** Pro Tip – Repeat a Post to Book Meetings **

See Figure 4 – Pre-conference meeting schedule sample.

- Website / landing pages
    - Once attendees are aware that you will be participating in the show, making it easy for them to book a meeting with you via a QR code that leads to a landing page can start ROE momentum for both parties. You may even run a pre-contest or talk about your co-located happy hour.
    - These landing pages should also be included in any pre-show outbound email campaigns.
- Contact / attendee lists
    - In some cases, show companies may sell lists as part of their packages that you can use before and after the event.
        - More and more of these lists do not include email addresses, so you may need a person to use some software to find these addresses — your marketing team knows of a few on the market. In the case where the show list exceeds 500 attendees, it may make sense to pare the list to a manageable number to run a pre-show campaign or several campaigns.
        - Parsing categories that can become headers in your spreadsheet: Location, Geography, Personas (Executive, Technical, Role-based), Company, Customers, Prospects, Partners, Size (Revenue, Employees), Known/Unknown
        - Business development representatives can use lists as a great resource to call from to schedule meetings at the event for brand ambassadors.

- Show apps
  - Marketing and brand ambassadors should take advantage of the show app, which is usually free and interactive! They even encourage you to say something ... see the bottom of the pictures in Figure 15 – Show app samples — *"What's on your mind, Paul?"*
    - The show app is an easy way to break the ice and introduce yourself to people 1-2 weeks before the event. It allows you to:
      - Make "noise" about your product and message.
      - Be "you" by sharing a picture of some hobby that you are involved with, or even introduce your pet by saying, "Fido will miss me when I'm at the event," on the wall of the app.
      - Make connections — you can meet people virtually, and then it is so much nicer and easier to connect in real life.

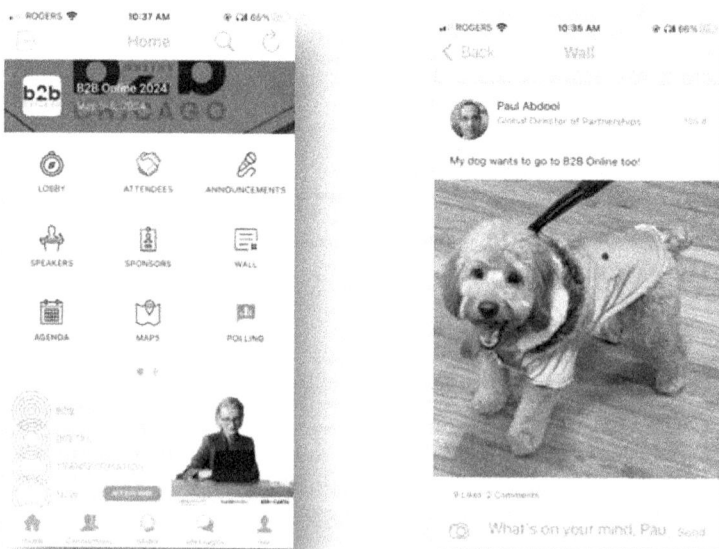

Figure 15 – Show app samples

Please note:

The show app is a very good item to sponsor. It is highly visible because it often has the names of all the attendees and speakers, and an event schedule, plus it often includes notifications that are selling your company every time a notification is sent.

- Examples of notification types: Keynote is about to speak, coffee break number 1 is open, lunch is ready, happy hour starts soon

** Pro Tip – Block Time for Follow-Ups **

Block two to three days, seven business days after the event, to follow up with prospective clients and book meetings.

The apps usually have an attendee list section and a messages section. Use the show app to remember all of the people you connected with before and during the event. It will make it easier for you to follow up. These allow you to remember key conversations and follow-up items.

Why is this important?

- It allows you to personalize follow-up messages, which will increase your:
    - o Meetings booked numbers
    - o Demo numbers
    - o Qualified lead numbers
    - o More importantly ... your Return on Event!
- Some sample fictitious messages from a show app's messages section:
    - o Joe Y — Company A
        - "Great to meet another Canadian in the e-commerce arena."
    - o Sue Z — Company B
        - "It was great to meet you at the hotel bar. I look forward to the demo we talked about having in a couple of weeks."
    - o John E — Company C
        - "Partner Y is here, and they want to bring Customer N by your booth at 10:30 a.m. tomorrow."
- More on this in Chapter 5 in the Post-show Follow-Ups section.

Lists and Sales Intelligence Platforms

One savvy and economical move is to use last year's attendees list if you are going back to the same event. Typically, people get into an event rhythm and show up at the same event again. So, the list will still be significant. You can also leverage some tools like Cognism, ZoomInfo or Apollo, to name a few, to enrich your lists with critical information and to remain compliant with evolving international privacy laws (GDPR, CCPA, Do-Not-Call lists, etc.).

Shipping

Give yourself time to ship your goods to the event. If you ordered anything for the show, get it shipped to you first to ensure quality, then add that to your overall shipment.

** Pro Tip – Brand New Booth **

Set up your booth in your office prior to shipping it. Make sure everything is in good condition. You should have all components in your hands at least four weeks before shipping.

Miscellaneous Items to Pack

There are a few things you will need in order to move your equipment, prepare it for the show and return it back to the office.

- Duct tape
  - This is the super tool to hide and fix many things
- Packing tape
  - To reseal all of your boxes
- Electrical ties
  - To bundle and hide wires for a nice, finished look, and for safety
- Screwdriver
  - A multi-head screwdriver to make minor repairs
- Knife
  - To cut packing tape or to open brochure packaging and boxes
- Extra phone chargers or portable battery chargers
  - Important for:
    - Lead retrieval scanners
    - LinkedIn
    - Texting people
    - Calling team members or acquaintances
- Mints
  - You and your team and others want to be fresh and confident for conversations
  - Especially after coffee and lunch breaks
- Ladder or stool
  - For the folks that are vertically challenged
  - Of course, if you are driving take these, but it may not make sense if you are shipping these items
- Dolly
  - Not the famous singer; this is a two- or four-wheel apparatus to help you roll in heavy items instead of carrying them
  - If the show is at a hotel, they will have carts you can use; they are usually by the check-in; another reason to go early!

** Pro Tip – Pre-Print Return Labels **

Pre-print return labels for all of your boxes and equipment and include them in one of the boxes.

Chapter 4 – At the Event

The Day Before – Go Early

Going early allows you to take your time and be prepared. It gives you time to learn where everything is, so you can be efficient with your movements from place to place, and can be a host for your prospective customers. It is the beginning of showing leadership, confidence, credibility and support.

** Pro Tip – Be the Guide on the Elevator **

If you know what floor the exhibit floor is on, the hall where the keynote is presenting, or where the lunch or happy hour are, you have something to say on the elevator.

When you know the lay of the land, you already have a minor competitive advantage over the people that are rushing. You are in a calmer state. You can walk with purpose and poise. All of these elements create a presence and aura that others will sense.

Booth Setup

Set up your booth as early as possible.

If you are able to set it up yourself, ensure you know how to get your booth and supporting paraphernalia to the show floor. For example, learn where the loading doors or elevators are. Scout out the route first to ensure the easiest way to transport your booth supplies.

Once you have everything on the show floor, set it up to ensure it all works:

- Booth and/or displays
- Computer monitors
- Power cords
- Tablecloths
- Brochures
- Giveaways (keep in box but know the layout)
  - Keep prizes out of sight when booth is unattended, as competitors, show staff or union workers may take some when you are not there

** Pro Tip – Set Up an Ambassador or Team Group Chat **

This is critical for general communication but also to align subject matter experts with last-minute appointments or to pull critical players into conversations when they are in a different part of the building.

Register early

Be one of the first to register. You avoid the long lines, and you get your badge early. This allows others to recognize that you are part of the event, and you instantly have something to chat about. "Where did you get your badge?" is a frequently asked question.

** Pro Tip – Use the QR Code at Registration **

Many shows provide you with an email that has a QR code you can scan to expedite your registration and the badge printing process. Use it.

Once you get your badge, shorten it by tying a knot in it at the back.

Why?

Short answer:

- People won't be forced to look down at your belly button to remember your name.
- It is more visible.

Long answer:

- See Appendix F – Badge Positioning and Etiquette

Badge codes

Focus on the codes that matter to you. This is critical when the event gets busy.

Typically, there are two to three types of badges:

- Attendee
- Sponsor
- Show Staff

However, at larger events or where they segment the attendees more, there is a list of badge codes. This granularity can help you if you are your firm's booth organizer or an attendee. These are visual cues to allow you to distinguish between key players.

** Pro Tip – Take a Picture of the Badge Codes **

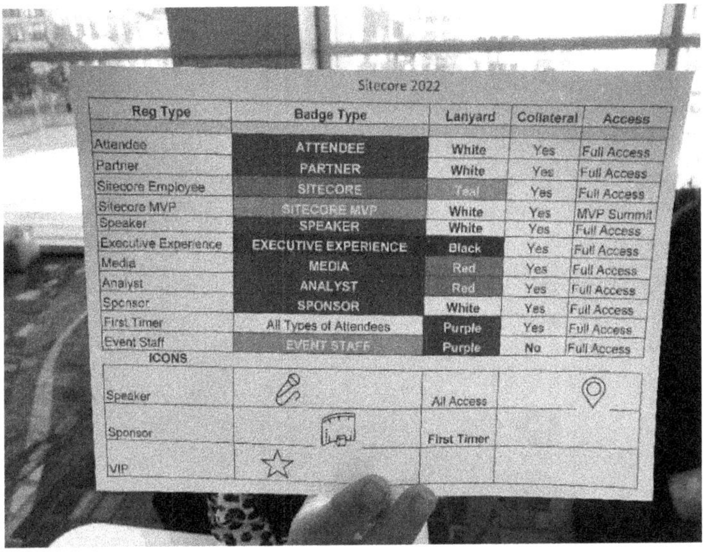

Sitecore 2022

Reg Type	Badge Type	Lanyard	Collateral	Access
Attendee	ATTENDEE	White	Yes	Full Access
Partner	PARTNER	White	Yes	Full Access
Sitecore Employee	SITECORE	Teal	Yes	Full Access
Sitecore MVP	SITECORE MVP	White	Yes	MVP Summit
Speaker	SPEAKER	White	Yes	Full Access
Executive Experience	EXECUTIVE EXPERIENCE	Black	Yes	Full Access
Media	MEDIA	Red	Yes	Full Access
Analyst	ANALYST	Red	Yes	Full Access
Sponsor	SPONSOR	White	Yes	Full Access
First Timer	All Types of Attendees	Purple	Yes	Full Access
Event Staff	EVENT STAFF	Purple	No	Full Access

ICONS

Speaker		All Access	
Sponsor		First Timer	
VIP			

Figure 16 – Sample badge codes

Opening Day ... Game Time!

The day has arrived. You have executed your pre-event marketing plan well, and now you are in the marketplace. It's game time!

As a marketer or brand ambassador, you are usually there before the attendees arrive. You must set up any last-minute items; you need to prepare your booth or stand to host the eager attendees.

Remember, your mission is to gather leads, get the word out or solidify your brand and to learn.

When you are assigned to participate in a conference, you should be honored. You have been identified as a brand ambassador, a subject matter expert or simply a person that your company is confident will represent them well. Your company trusts you: make them proud.

And don't forget ... you are representing yourself too! Your future can be affected by this event. It could mean a new prospect or partnership, your next job or a job 10 years from now. You never know who is observing you.

Be yourself, enjoy and be great!

** Pro Tip – Brand Ambassador and Booth Never-Evers **

1. Never be late for booth duty.
2. Never leave the booth unattended or leave without informing colleagues.
3. Never sit (not all of you), or only sit while meeting with a prospective customer or partner.
4. Never eat or drink in the booth except during a happy hour.
5. Never let the booth get cluttered, untidy or disorganized. Hide your bags behind booth or under skirted tables.
6. Never ignore prospects by forming a cozy cluster and chatting with colleagues.
7. Never close off potential conversations by crossing your arms and looking unapproachable.
8. Never stand with your back to the aisle.
9. Never use inappropriate language, complain about the show or about being at the show.
10. Never say "Can I help you?" (See Chapter 10 — Conversation Topics – What Do I Say When I Meet Strangers?)
11. Never badmouth your competitors.
12. Never wear new shoes or high heels — bring two pairs of shoes to alternate for multi-day shows.

** Pro Tip – Leveraging Show App **

- Use the show app to bring attention to your company and yourself.
  - Why?
    - This makes you more recognizable and approachable, since people are already "meeting" you virtually.
- It also allows you to reach out to people via the app.
  - Why?
    - Momentum is building and people are now in motion, so this allows you to get them to make minor commitments, like a short meeting in the lobby.
    - See Figure 17 – Show app communication samples.

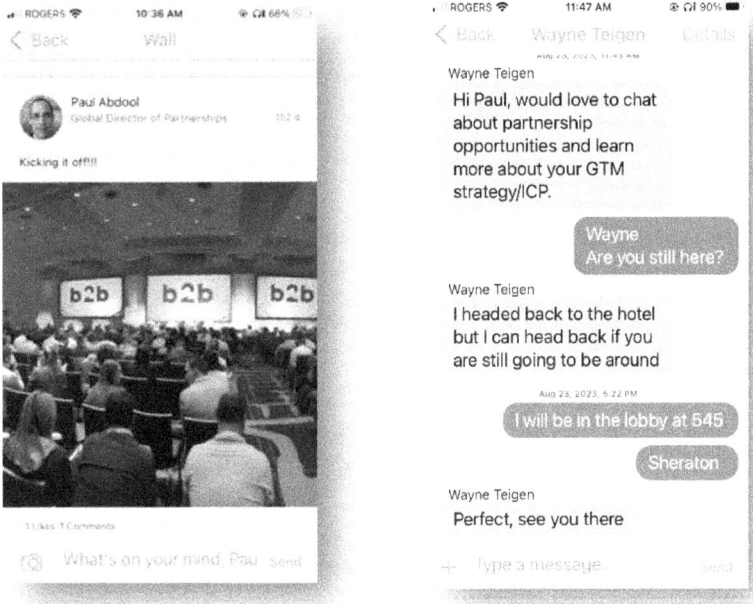

Figure 17 – Show app communication samples

63

The Exhibit Zone

This is the playing field, where the hustle hits reality. It's not the size and expense of the booth; it's how you work in and around it. Activities need to be choreographed and sometimes even ad-libbed. What you have practiced will be executed. Some people come by it naturally; others need to practice to fine-tune their booth skills. All of this needs to happen ahead of the conference exhibit floor opening. Before the audience of prospects, customers, consultants and analysts arrive, your team needs to be ready.

Preparing your Brand Ambassadors for the Action Zone

Your hunters and gatherers (sales executives, account managers, partner managers) need to keep active, be conversational and bring people into the booth to see demos from your subject matter experts (SMEs) or to discuss your products and services with key executives.

Of course, this is easier said than done. All the pre-show marketing, your efforts on the show app, your workout in the morning, attending in-show and industry networking events and a little bit of hustle will pay off.

To ensure success, your brand ambassador team must be trained. They must also understand the mission. When they understand this, they will be ahead of most other people taking up space in their booths or reading emails on their phones.

Brand Ambassador Training

Before the show starts, a team meeting needs to take place. A general agenda is below:

- Booth tour
    - Review the messaging and what you will be showing (demo)
    - Bag hiding places
    - Prizes and giveaway rules
- Booth hours review
    - Breaks
- Roles and the handoff procedure
    - Hunters and gatherers
    - Subject matter experts
    - Executives
    - Speakers at the event
- People expected to visit the booth
    - Customers, prospects, partners, executives

- Data and documentation methodology
  - Minimum data capture
  - Definitions of leads — A, B, C
    - Example — A Lead = In market; buying within three months; meeting next week
  - Badge scanners (e.g., SmartSource Leads app)
    - Review the application, so nobody is fumbling when visitors come to the booth
  - Business cards
- The 30-second elevator pitch
  - Incorporates your firm's one-line description and the "secret sauce"
- Case study familiarity
  - Know 10 customers that you do business with
  - Know two to five case studies based on use cases

Know and Share the Mission

Prior to the show, you need to define what success looks like. At the show it needs to be repeated and shared with the entire team. Key performance indicators (KPIs) can be any or all of the following:

- Meetings booked pre-show / meetings attended at show
- Demos completed — companies and people
- Badges scanned
- Meetings booked post-show
- Opportunities produced / deals closed
- Partnerships added
- Intelligence gathered

The Action Zone

Where do you work? You must work **outside** of your booth during the show!

(See Figure 18 – Action Zone: Working outside your booth.)

** Pro Tip - Work Outside Your Booth **

There is no room for laziness. Your team — and yes, it is a team sport — must work the ACTION ZONE. This is the area around and near your booth. It could be the aisle (action zone is at least halfway across the aisle), the food and beverage station or anywhere on or off the show floor.

The zone depends on the layout of the show floor, but here are some general guidelines.

- Guidelines for handoffs and assignments:
  - Prospects / customers 🏃
  - Hunters and gatherers 👤 👤 (usually sales staff or partner managers)
    - Stand outside your booth or by beverage and food stations and bring people to your booth
  - Directors of inbound prospects 👤 (the "booth czar" — usually marketing)
    - Direct inbound prospects to SMEs for deeper discussions
  - Subject matter experts (SMEs) 👤 (solution engineers or founders or executives)
    - Stand or sit inside booth or by the demonstration station
- There must be a clear handoff plan to manage the attendee's journey.
  - The hunters and gatherers need to know who to hand off the attendee to.
  - This is done with a brief discovery question or two, or even using the badge scanning app with preloaded questions.
  - Introduce the attendee to the appropriate person and provide the SME or executive with a brief background of your discussion — nobody wants to waste time repeating themselves.
  - Once the attendee is in good hands, ensure that more than one person is listening to take notes to support the SME or executive.

- o Ensure that the next steps are agreed upon and clear; this will make it easier to follow up with them using their preferred timeline.
- o When they leave, rank and document the conversation in greater detail; it is worth the extra 60 seconds while the conversation is fresh in your head.

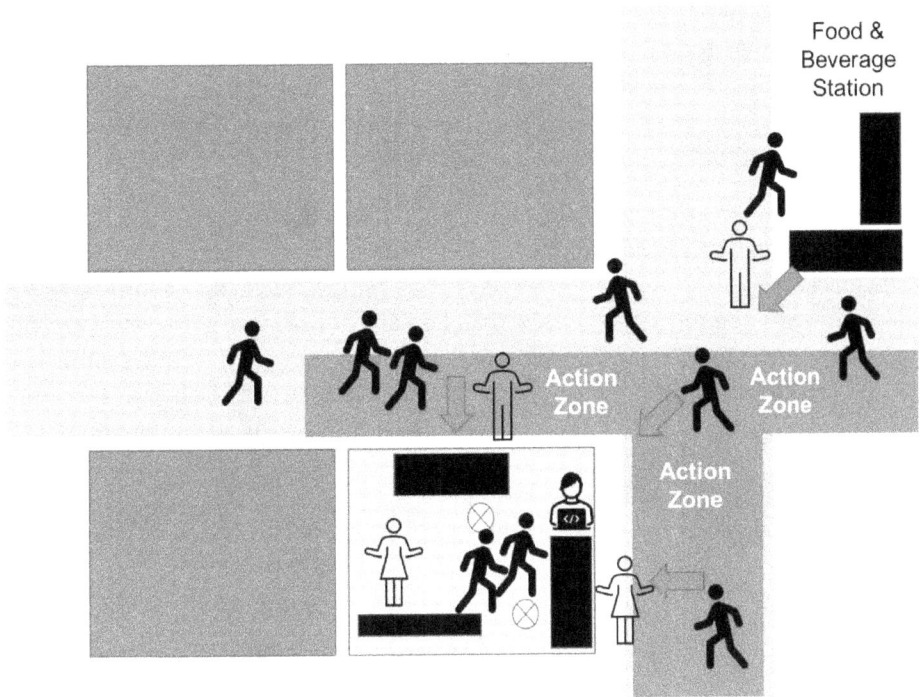

Food &
Beverage
Station

Action
Zone

Action
Zone

Action
Zone

Figure 18 – Action Zone: Working outside your booth

Besides great icebreaker questions and some good hustle, people having fun attracts others to your booth. A mix of high energy, smart people and some eye-catching things will draw people in. The pre-show invitations and incentives, colorful giveaways, the speaker representing your firm from a session earlier in the day: all of these tools must be used.

Of course, don't forget the theme of the book — *From Workout to Last Call*.

What did you do the night before to meet people?

Did you take advantage of the happy hour the night before or activities in the morning or go for a morning workout?

See Chapter 7 – Types of Networking Moments for ideas for frontloading your booth pipeline to attract more people to your place of business. People are more likely to stop if they are acquainted with you or your company's brand and feel that they are learning, not being sold to.

For example, at three different shows, I went for a morning workout. I did my thing, and inevitably you will see other people in the gym. Usually the "go-getters" — senior people and intense individuals — will be the personas in the gym. These people will also make it to breakfast, and in all likelihood they will explore the show floor. You don't need to speak with them in the gym, although you can if it is appropriate. However, you do need to note them. They may even be wearing a company shirt to work out in.

As these people walk down the aisle or grab their protein and smoothie from the food and beverage station, you instantly have something in common. These people will take 60-90 seconds out of their day to talk with someone they shared a gym with. On two different occasions, with coffee and snack in hand, people watched demos in my booth after we crossed paths in the gym. This is just one example of taking advantage of the networking moments — Section 2 in this book.

As I was thinking about this section of the book, I thought to myself, who can I reach out to, to share a story with you? I asked Karri Parks, Senior Director, Digital Experience, at Presidio, to share how we met and her thoughts on networking.

"I became comfortable with networking when I realized it means having genuine conversations based on shared interests, not forced interactions. First, identify your interests, not who you want to meet or your future job goals. Engage in activities that recharge you and notice who's around you; this is your tribe. Your tribe has common interests but can also introduce you to new circles and experiences.

For example, I prioritize daily workouts and easily talk about fitness. At a conference in Chicago, using the hotel's gym led to a conversation with Paul in the exhibit hall about my workout, forming an instant connection!

That led to a conversation about my goals for the conference, an introduction to a potential partner and a software demo that I probably wouldn't have experienced if not for the shared gym connection. This is the power of networking!"

Karri Parks
Senior Director, Digital Experience, Presidio

These stories are countless out there, whether it is a workout, a matching suitcase in the lobby or a t-shirt with your favorite team on it. As stated above, there is a connection between humans that initiates a conversation to learn more about the person and stimulates our desire to help them out.

Long Game – Working Outside Your Booth

BCC Software was a long-time partner of mine when I was at Ricoh Americas and Solimar Systems, Inc. At the time, my customer from the Colorado State Printer (Mike Lincoln — RIP) and I ran in some of the same industry circles, and he viewed me as a trusted advisor.

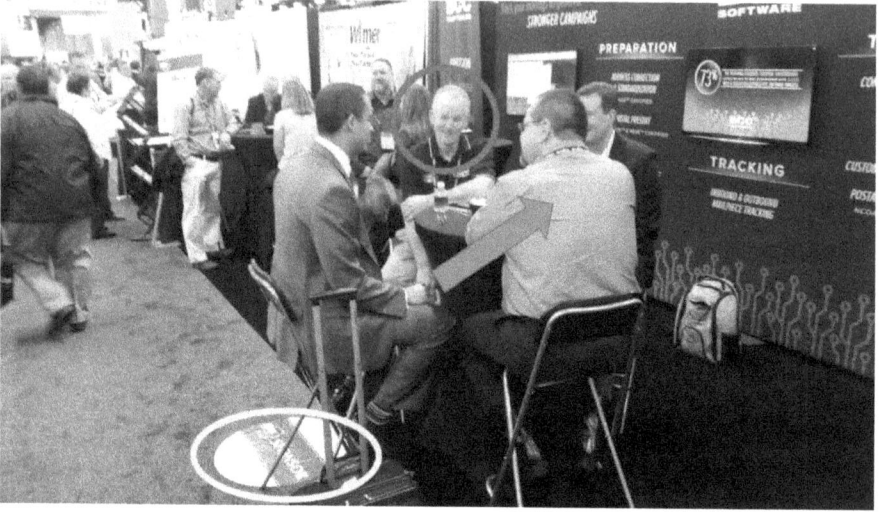

Figure 19 – Taking a prospect to a partner's booth

The quote below from Mike Lincoln (arrow), former Colorado State Printer[24], shows how we both used our social capital to help our firms and partners.

---

[24] From a LinkedIn recommendation about my support to Mike Lincoln.

70

"When I was looking to move Colorado's Integrated Document Solutions to the next level, I had some major strategic decisions to make and some complex business processes that fell outside my wheelhouse. I needed a business partner who would be able to fill the gaps in my knowledge base and provide a support role as we moved forward. Paul provided both the macro and micro details that I required, not only through his own expertise but also by bringing some great partners to the table to make our vision a viable reality."

Mike Lincoln

As Mike stated, he was trying to solve a problem. I believed BCC (partner manager circled in dark grey) could help due to some integrations between our firms. At the time of this photo at the National Postal Forum (NPF), we all agreed to have a joint discovery meeting a few weeks later with three partners (Solimar Systems, Racami and BCC Software) to map out the challenges in detail and create an overall solution to update Mike's operation.

What you see in the picture above and what you don't is important to note.

What you see:

- The meeting
- The sponsorship — credibility (circled in white)

What you don't see:

- The three other events that were attended earlier in the year to build credibility with the prospect
- Knowing the prospect's problem ahead of time (initial discovery)
- The preparation before the show to get the prospect to the booth; emails and phone calls
- Understanding the prospect's schedule
- Attending the prospect's presentation in a breakout room
- The escorting of the prospect to the booth from the food and beverage area

My point is simple. You have to work outside of your booth before, during and after the show.

Some organizations are intentionally shaping the way knowledge transfer, sales, and face-to-face interactions take place. They are applying the same approach I described earlier with Mike, but on a larger scale — identifying thought leaders, connecting them with end-users (customers and operators), and strategically integrating the right sponsors or vendors. Some of them will even have "meeting runners" to get the person to your meeting if they are distracted, just like I escorted Mike from the food and beverage area to the booth in Figure 19 – Taking a prospect to a partner's booth.

Some events facilitate meetings that would be nearly impossible to secure on your own. They take it a step further by providing sponsors with attendee lists in advance, enabling initial discovery calls before the in-person meeting. This goes beyond just an introduction — it integrates directly into your go-to-market strategy. You have control over who you meet, allowing you to pre-qualify decision-makers before confirming meetings. For example, if your package includes 10 meetings, you can shortlist 20 prospects, conduct preliminary calls, and refine your list — keeping the strongest opportunities and swapping out others as needed. This model maximizes your Return on Event (ROE), accelerates your sales cycle and streamlines the buyer's journey.

Photo and Video Content

Record content that you can use for both marketing and post-show follow-ups.

What you need to focus on is carving out time to do this before, during and after the event. When things get busy, this is an area that can go astray. You cannot take too many pictures or too much video footage.

** Pro Tip - Minimum Photo and Video Content **

- Photos
  - Empty booth after it is set up
  - Busy booth — with people talking to your brand ambassadors or watching demos
  - Keynote presentation
  - Your company's presenters
  - Competitor's presentation — the people in it; note the question askers
  - Sponsorships — cups, signs, giveaways, keynotes, lunches
  - Be creative
- Videos
  - People entering the show floor after the keynote or when the floor opens
  - Your company's presenters
  - Brand ambassadors in action
  - Interviews — key subjects, show commentary
    - Planned
    - Ad hoc
  - Testimonials
  - Happy hours / mixers
  - Be creative

Post live from the show and/or send pictures back to the marketing team for live social media posts.

Use the following to create buzz before and after the shows:

- The show's hashtags (#)
- Your company's social media handles (URLs/nicknames)
- Your social media handles

Repurposing Content

Content repurposing is the process of reusing existing content in a different format to reach new audiences. It's a key part of content marketing strategies.

Why repurpose content?

- Saves time and resources
  - Repurposing content is more efficient than creating content from scratch.
- Improves SEO (search engine optimization)
  - Repurposed content can help improve search engine visibility.
- Increases audience reach
  - Repurposing content allows you to reach more people in different formats.

"Events are not just opportunities for networking and learning — they are the perfect backdrop for powerful content creation. Static content doesn't scale; it blends into the mundane. But change the setting, capture the vibrant atmosphere, and leverage the collective expertise around you, and your message gains unparalleled reach.

With just a smartphone and a microphone, you can transform any event into a dynamic content engine, creating engaging material that resonates far beyond the event itself. Think of events as your stage, where every interaction and every backdrop become part of a compelling narrative that keeps delivering value long after the event has ended."

Matthew McQueeney

How to repurpose content?

- Republish content on different platforms, such as LinkedIn or Medium.
- Create new formats. For example, turn show videos into webinar introductions.
- Extract quotes from event blog or video posts or other content to create an e-book.
- Use old images as backgrounds for posts.
- Create snippets from event video content.

All of the above can be used for post-event follow-ups and can enrich messaging to differentiate yourself from the noise of everyone else's post-event follow-up activities.

Leave Late

Leaving an event after the prospects have left allows you to maximize your investment.

Booth Breakdown and Move Out

On the last day of the show in the morning, or the day before, all exhibitors should get an Exhibitor Move Out Instruction Sheet if the show is medium in size or greater. These will give you details on how to ship your booth out if you are not taking it out yourself. In many cases, you will be shipping your booth back to your marketing department or to headquarters. They should pre-print return labels for all of your boxes and equipment.

There is no prize for being the first vendor to leave (See Figure 20 – Empty booth). This booth was across from me. They left one hour early. This may be the only time that someone had time to visit your booth. You might be leaving money on the table!

Figure 20 – Empty booth

If budget and timing allow, you can ensure that everything is put away neatly and ready for the next event. This will keep equipment from being damaged, so you don't have to waste time replacing parts or pieces prior to your next event.

In addition, you can visit current customers or prospects in the area. In today's mostly remote working environment, a post-event team meeting at a place in the city that most of your team probably haven't had the opportunity to visit is both bonding and a nice way to say thank you for their hard work.

Chapter 5 – After the Event

The Debrief Meeting

This is another calm state that will support strategizing on your next steps. The debrief meeting is a great best practice to gather details while the event is fresh in people's minds. Leads can be cleansed and prioritized. Post-show ROE (ROI and payback period) documents/calculators can be populated, which will inform upcoming financial forecasts.

Post-show Follow-Ups

As they say, the fortune is in the follow-up. An event is not the end; it is just the beginning of a brand new pipeline or a part of your sales cycle with a prospect or a customer. Your strategy to maintain momentum and transform discussions into tangible results should already be developed and ready to execute with Marketing, the Sales team, Product, Partner Managers and Customer Success.

Don't be in a rush to follow up as soon as you get back to the office. Let everyone catch their breath and get back into their regular grooves.

There may be a few exceptions based on notes gathered at the show, but as a rule, do not follow up with attendees, unless they have explicitly requested it, within two to four business days after the event. The attendees have been away from their family and their offices for a while. They are tired and have some catching up to do as well.

The A[25] level leads should be designated to the Sales team that met with them at the show, or if the prospect is in their territory or vertical. They should create specific, personal follow-up messages or call them directly to book meetings. Emails and voicemails should include specifics from memorable moments at the show and should mention the business problems that you promised to follow up on.

The B[26] and C[27] level leads should be well orchestrated with Marketing and Revenue Operations teams. You should have your post-show messaging and email

---

[25] In market to buy within your average sales cycle, the project is approved, and the budget is established or actively being developed (i.e., taking proposals, or an RFP will be issued shortly).

[26] Leads that are not in market or still forming budgets and committees for the future.

[27] Leads that were from show lists that fit your ideal customer profile (ICP).

sequences set up prior to the event. You may want to adjust these based on personal conversations or any relevant groundbreaking information that you heard.

Populate your customer relationship management (CRM) with lists received from the event or lists that you created with your team. The first of three to four email sequences should be sent the Monday following the show. Block time in your calendar seven business days after the event for follow-up calls and meeting setting with all email recipients.

Do not stop following up until you have tried multiple times.

People are busy, it's not you, it's their schedules. Also note that conference seasons are typically in the spring and fall, and some people, especially decision-makers, may be participating in multiple events over an eight-week period, which can make it difficult to book and take meetings. Be persistent and provide valuable information about the subject they were interested in at the show.

** Pro Tip – The Follow-up Card **

Some of the most successful people I know have sent a follow-up card or something in the MAIL! Yes, a good old envelope in a mailbox. USPS[28] used to call it the "mail moment" — that moment when you open up something different.

Here is an excerpt from a LinkedIn post by Antonio Neves[29] regarding thank-you cards:

"I've been a handwritten thank-you guy since college.

Why? Because I never wanted to be 'deletable.'

A text gets swiped. An email gets archived.

But a card is real.

You can feel it.

It takes the effort of going to the post office.

Today, buy some stationery.

Write a thank-you card. Mail it.

Do it because it's a simple way to make a difference.

Do it because people deserve (and need) to feel something real.

And do it because some things, like a thank-you card, survive."

Antonio Neves, author, *Stop Living on Autopilot*

---

[28] United States Post Office
[29] https://theantonioneves.com/

A friend of mine, Skip Henk, former president and CEO of Xplor International[30], has also sent thousands of thank-you cards. In Figure 21 – Thank-you note sample, you will see two of the many that I have received as a board member, an exhibitor or an attendee.

They were all appreciated and treasured.

As Antonio stated, "they are not deletable." For the cynics out there, yes, they can be recycled, but there is still that "mail moment" when you open up that envelope that is different than the millions of emails, texts and other digital communications you will receive.

Ask yourself this question: does your mom want a thank-you text on Mother's Day for being a great mom, or a nice card?

You know the right answer.

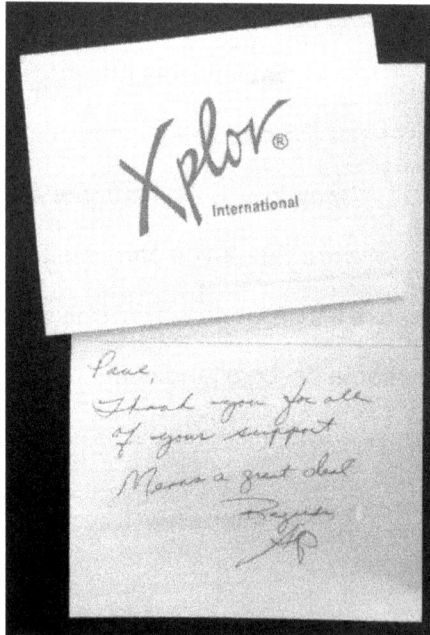

Figure 21 – Thank-you note sample

---

[30] Xplor International - https://xplor.org/

One of my favorite follow-ups of all time was from Sveinbjörn Hjálmarsson. He owned an Icelandic printing operation called Umslag. After a conference, he used to send follow-up notes and Christmas cards. In a few cases, he put a little something in them. In this case, it was a coaster: see Figure 22 – Coasters in a thank-you card. As you can see, I have had this on my desk for many years ... and many coffees. It is an example of a useful, easy and economical follow-up item.

He was consistent and the marketing message was persistent as it sat on my desk ... and it was thoughtful too!

Figure 22 – Coasters in a thank-you card

** Pro Tip - The Power of Associations **

Networking and professional associations can lead to many other activities that can build your social capital, like being asked to write articles in industry magazines or participating in podcasts. After meeting Leslie Greenwood via a group of go-to-market (GTM) professionals called Pavilion, I got to know her by participating in a few online Pavilion events. We stayed in touch as she transitioned to become the founder of Chief Evangelist (https://thechiefevangelist.com/). One day I reached out to her since I was going to be in her hometown of Dallas, Texas, in a few weeks. We started exchanging emails, and she invited me to be a guest on her People Powered Podcasts[31]. Listen to the episode[32] to hear the whole story and to hear some other networking tips.

There are a few takeaways from above:

1. Associations are a great place to meet and get to know people in your industry.
2. Stay in touch occasionally with your network, especially if you will be in their hometown. Wouldn't the world be a better place if everyone did ... I digress.
3. Listening to each other and supporting people without transactions in mind is a great way to stay in touch.
4. Get involved not just as a participant but as a volunteer or a board member to really grow your credibility and social capital.

---

[31] The People Powered Community Podcast shares inspiring stories of go-to-market professionals who use their superpowers to create strong and lasting connections with their community.

[32] https://www.iheart.com/podcast/269-the-people-powered-communi-112359178/episode/020-paul-abdool-building-powerful-122205158/

Communicating with Loved Ones

This may seem a little odd to put in this book. As I mentioned in the introduction, *From Workout to Last Call* is a motto for always being ready to represent you and your company. However, giving your all at work can feel unfair to those at home. They want your all as well.

During the Event

Someone is at home, holding down the fort. They may have less on their mind because they are going through their regular routine, except it may be more work if you are away. They are thinking about you, especially if they feel more tired because their load has increased (e.g., children, school/daycare drop-offs, lunches/dinners, etc.). They may also perceive your conference as a fun getaway, almost vacation-like, particularly if you are off to a sunny destination or a big city.

So, first you need to level set that it is work. Events can have perks like going to great restaurants, or there may be some fun elements like attending sporting events or a few minutes to enjoy some sun by a pool, so don't rub it in. Don't take too many fun pictures and post them. Take tasteful group shots with partners and customers for professional posts like LinkedIn, but put down the beer and cocktails.

Let them know that you are busy at these events from the time you wake up to the time you go to sleep. Establish a time to communicate with them ahead of time. Here are some factors to consider that may make their perfect times to communicate incongruent with your perfect times:

- Time zones
- Their schedules at home
- Work
- After-school events
- Established meetings
- Ad hoc meetings

** Pro Tip – Suggest Replacing Calls Home with Pictures **

As they say, a picture is worth a thousand words. In addition, there are no time constraints, background noise at airports or busy lobbies, and no rushing off because you have only a few minutes. It demonstrates that you are thinking about them and sharing your day. It may also stimulate future discussions for when you get home.

Another "I'm thinking of you" component are age-appropriate trade show take-home gifts. My kids and wife always appreciated such items when I got home.

Whether you are an attendee, exhibitor or sponsor, you will inevitably have a moment to walk through the exhibit area learning about what organizations have to offer. During this time, it is nice to pick up one or two things that your family or pet will appreciate. It shows them you were thinking about them and even conversing about them with the person you acquired it from. It could be any of the following:

- Stuffed animal
- Notebook
- Phone charger / back up battery
- Wipes for glasses
- Coffee cup
- Golf ball
- Chew toy
- Wine travel mug / bottle stopper

Don't forget to make sure you have a bit of room in your bag to get these items home.

What Do You Do When You Get Home?

When you get home, do you have a conference hangover?

Even if you are tired, give your loved ones the same energy that you exuded while at the event. If someone is going to be awake when you get home, drink a coffee or your favorite caffeine-filled beverage on your way home. You must provide them with at least one or two hours of energy, depending on the time of day and the events at home.

Walk in the door and dig deep with energy:

- Hugs
- Chores (dinner — e.g., cook or order in, do dishes, change diapers)
- Listen (complaints — i.e., how hard it was while you were away)
- Play with kids
- Share your gifts

What not to talk about!

- All the fun you had … unless you are asked … and even so proceed with caution. Don't go overboard!
- Expensive surf and turf dinners
- Box seats to the Lakers game
- The great weather; the beach or mountain scenery from your room

The bottom line … they are your "last call."

Section 2 – Networking Nexus

As mentioned in the title of the book, *From Workout to Last Call* implies an "always on" mentality while at an event. This section provides a collection or nexus of ideas and networking concepts to prepare you to take advantage of the numerous types of networking moments you will experience.

Make networking a priority!

"I used to think conferences were a waste of time, until I realized I was doing it wrong.

Conferences are a wonderful place to get face-to-face with many people in a very short period of time.

You will grow, you will meet new people, and you will have so much more fun when you do it for yourself.

So, make it a priority and attend at least one conference each year."

Martin Roth
Founder, martinroth.com

Chapter 6 – Show Up, Set Goals and Capture Data

Show Up!

It is worth repeating, ***From Workout to Last Call*** is analogous to always being ready to represent you and your company. The concept is simple: if you are awake, you should be working.

When I say working, I'm not saying you should always be selling or pitching your product, but you should be ready to network by showing up from sunrise to last opportunity to converse with someone.

Yes, it is exhausting.

Yes, you will leave tired.

Yes, you should give it your full effort to maximize your time and the investment that your company has made in this event.

So, how do you go about doing this? Keep reading.

Set Goals!

Set a goal — how many people do you want to meet?

Set a personal goal for how many people you want to, or should, meet to increase your network's capital. This could be as simple and as low as one person per networking opportunity, or it could be a daily goal of 10. There are no rules, except: do not be a solitary being for the whole event.

How are you going to know if you are meeting your goal?

Capture Data!

You must measure and document as much as you can! This is part of your Return on Event (ROE).

Write notes in your networking mini notebook as soon as you leave each conversation. I will discuss this more in the Minimum Data Capture section that follows.

** Pro Tip – Trust > Transactions **

Networking is not transactional. Networking may lead to future transactions. However, the intent is to establish trust and credibility to open doors that you don't even know you need to walk through yet.

Minimum Data Capture

If you are working all day, you will inevitably meet people. Unless you have a photographic or autobiographical memory, you need to capture data about the people you meet to refer to it later.

There are four things you need to capture:

- Name
- Company
- Contact information
- Something you will remember them by:
    - Your conversation — e.g., Where they are from, something they said, accent
    - What they were wearing — e.g., Red shirt, fedora, cowboy boots

Please note that this information has several purposes.

- The obvious one is that it is critical for your post-show follow-up.
- It is also important for in-event networking or, in other words, the other times you may run into them during the event.
    - This allows you to act like a host and introduce them to someone else at the event.
        - See Chapter 10 – Act Like You Are the Host

If these things make you feel uncomfortable, you are not alone. In fact, some studies show that over 75% of people are uncomfortable with networking, and that is without the "minimum data capture" component.

See Chapter 9 – Extraverts, Introverts and Ambiverts – Who Are You? You may not be a very outgoing person, which by the way is OK — more than OK, you be you. In fact, in the introvert section, you will learn why introverts can be better networkers than extraverts.

An easy way to capture someone's information, outside of grabbing a business card (which I believe will make a comeback) is to scan someone's LinkedIn profile. This is critical in a busy event. Maya Meyouhas, founder of MIM Marketing, created a great explanation of three easy ways to share your LinkedIn profile in the heat of in-real-life (IRL) personal data exchange.

Level 1: For beginner networkers

On your iPhone, long press the LinkedIn icon and select "Scan QR code." This brings you straight to the page with your QR code so anyone can scan it with their camera; no need to be in the LinkedIn app.

Level 2: For intermediate connectors

Take a screenshot of that LinkedIn QR page and set it as your lock screen for the duration of the event. This way, you don't even need to unlock your phone to share your LinkedIn details.

Level 3: For star networkers!

Copy the QR into Canva (or any other design software) and modify the visual to match your design aesthetic, then set that as your lock screen.

** Pro Tip – LinkedIn Level 3 **

I highly recommend Level 3 for an event! Sample below in Figure 23 – LinkedIn screen saver.

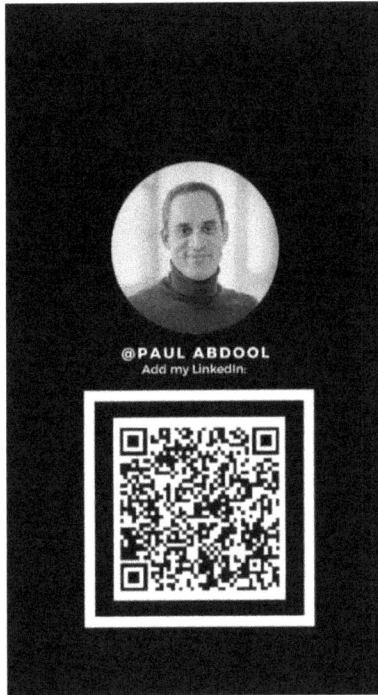

Figure 23 – LinkedIn screen saver

Meyouhas demonstrates all 3 levels in a step-by-step video:
https://youtu.be/ojwVHK_8Qn8?si=qmQHq-8QOVzWukZL.

** Pro Tip – Documenting Your New LinkedIn Connections **

I also suggest taking the time to write out all the names of the people you scanned to ensure that you add them to your follow-up list ... and yes, you have to follow up with some message when you return. The people you connected with need to remember you. Send them another message in about two weeks, even if you are not trying to sell them something. Get locked into their memory.

Chapter 7 – Types of Networking Moments

From sunrise to sunset, you need to get in the mindset of networking. The moments are numerous, and you need to stay focused and remain disciplined throughout the day. You won't be perfect, but if you are aware about the types of networking moments, they will remain in your subconscious and allow you to act in the moment.

> "The energy that comes from gathering in person — whether with partners, clients or colleagues — can't be replicated online. It's where ideas are sparked, trust is deepened, and plans come to life."
>
> Joe LaCroix
> Managing Director, PeakActivity

Workouts

Organized – Walks/Runs/Yoga Classes/Pickleball

Sometimes event planners will have organized morning workouts to kick-start the day. These are done for more than one reason. They can be another revenue source for the event; e.g., Optimity[33] sponsored the morning yoga class in Figure 24 – InsureTech Connect (ITC) – morning yoga event in Las Vegas. In the case of Optimity, it was on brand — "From Health to Wealth" … and I still have the yoga mat!

Figure 24 – InsureTech Connect (ITC) – morning yoga event in Las Vegas

---

[33] Optimity — https://www.myoptimity.com/

Financial or marketing benefits aside, workouts can be another way to stimulate networking.

Regardless of the reason, show up!

People remember people who attended these events. Usually, they are a subset of go-getters, or it is a hobby of a group of enthusiasts (e.g., runners, yogis).

Why attend, even if you are horrible at it?

- You will have an instant group of folks to network with at later functions.
- You will see people in more vulnerable states (e.g., no makeup, workout clothes), so when they see you again, they will be even more ready to talk.

An event I used to lead at one of my all-time favorite events, Xplor, was a morning run on the beach. This was another event sponsored by a firm I worked at, Solimar Systems, Inc. This idea is good for all levels of fitness, as long as you do an "out and back" — e.g., go north for 15 minutes and then turn around and go south for 15 minutes. The runners, walkers and strollers should all finish at the same place you started 30 minutes later.

Figure 25 – Xplor – Run, Walk or Stroll sponsor

Please note: Providing your team with workout gear is another economical form of marketing and another way to say thanks for being a brand ambassador. A few extras of these can also be good bonus booth giveaway items, especially for the folks that got out of bed and worked out!

Individual Workouts – Gym or Weight Room

High-powered, stressed and focused people work out in the morning.

The C-suite is up and at it, to prepare for their days and achieve their goals (e.g., marathon training, weight loss, training for event, lowering their stress).

So … show up and be seen!

> "Exercise is a crucial aspect of my routine as a leader. I prioritize physical activity to boost my endorphins and overall well-being … even when I am on the road."
>
> Pauline De Leon-Hutson
> AVP, Member Experience, Lakeland Credit Union

The difference between the gym and the organized events like the runs and yoga is the communication methodology. At the gym, you just nod and acknowledge people's presence, share equipment, be courteous by wiping down your machines and mats and hold the door for people.

Nothing more. Speak when spoken to.

But observe and remember who was there. Look for company logos on workout gear (e.g., t-shirts, water bottles). Inevitably, you will see these people at the event, and you will instantly have a conversation starter. For example, "I think I saw you at the gym this morning, are you training for something?"

Filling Your Cup

High-powered, stressed and focused people work out in the morning.

Extraverts need to fill their cup because they pour it out on a daily basis.

Introverts need to fill their cup because it feels like everyone is taking their limited energy.

Ambiverts: as usual, you are somewhere in the middle, and you need to fill your cup too!

** Pro Tip – Energy Generation **

Move in the morning, breathe in some fresh air or get your heart pumping. This will provide you with much needed oxygen and it will make you hungry and thirsty. Your body will force you to replenish itself at breakfast … where you might meet another person. See details on meals below.

Meals – Breakfast/Lunch/Dinner

Get out of bed or work out early enough to get to the event breakfast.

Show up!

If you are a hearty breakfast eater or have special dietary needs, eat breakfast somewhere else, early enough to show up for a beverage at the event's breakfast. Sit at a table with people you don't know and engage in light conversation.

- See Conversation Topics – What Do I Say When I Meet Strangers?

** Pro Tip – Table Layout Etiquette **

This may seem like a given if you have been to many formal functions; however, for those of you who have not frequented formal sit-down dinners, these tips may be a good reminder.

Why?

Although you want to be you, and I'm not judging … knowing some table etiquette avoids awkward moments, or you can be the person to support someone who is unsure. For example, "That bread plate on my left is mine," or "That glass on the right filled with water is the one you should drink out of."

Here are some general rules and ways to remember some dining etiquette. See the diagram in Figure 26 – Table layout and etiquette [34], for those who want the official layout.

- b (OK symbol made with your left hand) = bread plate on the left
- d (OK symbol made with your right hand) = drink glasses on the right
- Forks and knives — use them from the outside in
- Spoons — tricky: large = soup; small = coffee/tea stirrer or dessert; sometimes both

---

[34] Image credit: iMom — https://www.imom.com/printable/formal-table-place-setting-chart/

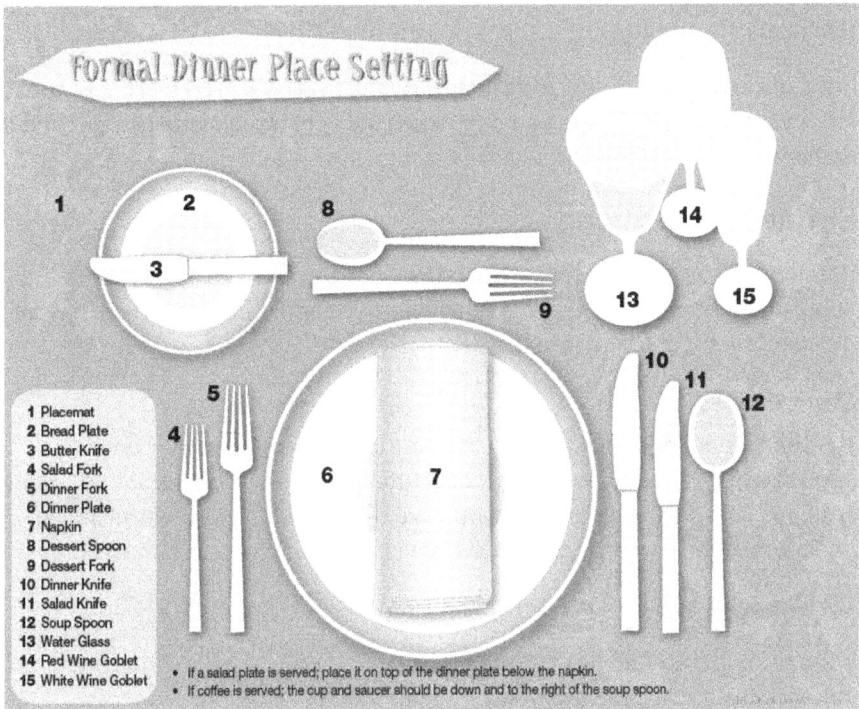

Formal Dinner Place Setting

1 Placemat
2 Bread Plate
3 Butter Knife
4 Salad Fork
5 Dinner Fork
6 Dinner Plate
7 Napkin
8 Dessert Spoon
9 Dessert Fork
10 Dinner Knife
11 Salad Knife
12 Soup Spoon
13 Water Glass
14 Red Wine Goblet
15 White Wine Goblet

• If a salad plate is served; place it on top of the dinner plate below the napkin.
• If coffee is served; the cup and saucer should be down and to the right of the soup spoon.

Figure 26 – Table layout and etiquette

Designated Mixers/Networking Time

This is the number one opportunity to network. It was designed for this purpose.

This is also an area of discomfort for many people. You will be OK.

Remember, it is networking. Work is the root of networking, so you may have to work at it a bit. It is not natural for everyone, and most people are not great at it. Many people can meet others or make some small talk, but can you take it to the next level and remember the people you met?

Chapter 10 – Networking Mindset and Movements will empower you with some techniques to employ.

Recently, I went to a conference in an industry that I was new to. I knew nobody. I felt uncomfortable and even a bit nervous, but I got myself into the right mindset and executed the steps and skills in Chapter 10.

Seminars/Sessions

Sessions are a great way to learn from leaders and your peers. You will also learn about your competition, the market, new trends and, most importantly, what your prospects want and who is in market.

General Sessions

These are good for understanding the tone of the event, and they provide information for future networking opportunities. Most people attend the general sessions, so sit beside someone you have never met and say hi. That is the minimum. If the person is responsive, you can ask, "Where are you from?"

That's it, that's all.

You can go further and deeper into a conversation if you want, if you are comfortable and if you have time before or after the session.

** Pro Tip – Take Notes **

Take notes; this will be good for the post-event report (See Appendix G – Post-Event Report) that is important to establish future budgets and demonstrate your professionalism when returning to your day job. This can also provide information for any town halls or other debrief presentations that you may have to do.

Your Competition's Sessions

While in the session, talk to active and engaged people as they exit. Go to their next session with them, or remember who they are and find them at other networking opportunities (e.g., coffee station, lunch tables, general sessions, etc.) and sit with them.

Also, do the following:

- Introduce yourself or note their badge and name.
- Find them on the show app and connect with them.

** Pro Tip – Cross-reference the Show App **

The show app may tell you a person's position at the company, and you may learn something else about them. You may have already reached out to them prior to the show, so check your CRM on your phone.

** Pro Tip – Intelligence Gathering in a Seminar **

Listen and take notes at your competitors' presentations. This is a free look inside their business. Study their messaging and tone. Listen to questions asked by prospective customers and note how your competitors answer them.

Look up the presenter on LinkedIn and see if they have connections with the other people in the room, especially the people asking questions or interacting with them.

Note the notetakers — they are in market or at least early in their research.

You may need to have more than one person from your company in the sessions:

- Product person
- Marketing person
- Salesperson
    - If you are one of the people who has a badge scanner app license, scan each new contact's badge with their permission.

Hotel Lobby

You are always on.

If you are waiting for anything (a colleague, a taxi, your luggage, etc.), talk to someone with a badge, or say hello if you recognize them from the event. I'm not saying go out of your way to make conversation, just be friendly if they are in your region — e.g., also waiting for someone, or at a taxi stand or the concierge.

Elevators

You board an elevator, or someone boards the elevator that you are in: you are now on! This event will happen multiple times at the event.

Figure 27 – Elevator filled with attendees

Look for the badges!

Most shows provide a name badge that is being held up by a colorful, branded lanyard. You can't miss it ... even if you haven't had a coffee yet.

This is a beacon of commonality: they are going where you are going at the same time you are. Elevators are gold for simple and easy icebreakers.

The "elevator pitch" can take two forms, and you have 30-90 seconds to deliver it, depending on the height of the hotel or conference center:

- Informal
    - "Hi, I see you are here for X show, where are you from?"

- Formal
    - "Hi, I see you are here for X show and you are with Y company, what do you do for them?"
    - This can lead to a longer, deeper conversation that may require you to continue to walk with this person after they exit the elevator. This can be awkward or uncomfortable because you may not know the person's immediate plans. So, unless you know the company or can provide some further color or insights, I do not recommend being formal in an elevator.
    - If both of you are waiting for an elevator and you use the formal opening, then you will have more time to converse about it prior to boarding the elevator.

Escalators

The cousin of the elevator is the long escalator. Apply the same methodology above.

> "Always take advantage of moments in life to connect with people around you, like extraordinarily long escalators. You never know the incredible people you'll meet and the relationships you build that last far beyond the moment."
>
> Marissa Buckley
> Founder, RevUp

Yes, Marissa Buckley and I met on escalators going in opposite directions at InsureTech Connect (ITC) in 2022. We have been in each other's networks since.

Be aware of your surroundings and always be on!

Buses to Events or Offsite Socials

You are locked in with two to six people around you for the duration of the ride. Usually, you are off to somewhere interesting and fun, so the atmosphere will be relaxed for the most part. Remember that the majority of people are uncomfortable, so make them feel comfortable or at least know that they may not want to start a discussion. You will probably have 15-20 minutes, depending on the distance to the event.

Go with the basics:

"Hi, where are you from?"

"What brought you to the conference?"

"What are you trying to get out of it?"

Depending on their mood or reception of your questions, end there or continue the conversation. Never force the conversation.

Washrooms

Tough one but still a potential place for networking.

"Hi" is all you should say.

** Pro Tip – Wash Your Hands Often **

Don't shake hands until you are outside. Of course, this assumes everyone has washed their hands.

Be observant about that. Stay healthy.

Chapter 8 – Tools for Networking

During the event, you should always be prepared with the following, but especially during the formal networking events/mixers.

Networking Checklist

- Your event badge
  - This is so important!
    - It gets you in places.
    - It allows others to spot you wherever you are.
    - It makes it easy for people to remember your name.
  - NOTE: Once you leave formal functions, remove your badge but don't lose it!

Figure 28 – The networking tool kit

- Gum/mints
  - Nobody wants to talk to someone with bad breath.
  - NOTE: These are often given away as tchotchkes/giveaways in a booth or stand even if you forget to buy some.
    - Fun fact: Why is it called a tchotchke (pronounced chach-key)?
      - Tchotchke comes from the Slavic word for trinket. Russian, Ukrainian, Polish and Belarusian each have their own very similar adaptations. It was later adopted into Yiddish slang as *tshatshke* and has long been used by Jewish Americans.
    - And ... another good conversation piece.
- Pen and mini notebook (or a page or two from a notebook)
  - You want to remember who you met if they don't have a business card or a way to get in touch with them later.
  - You also want to remember what you talked about for following up with them after the show. Especially if you learned something about a hobby or an upcoming business opportunity (e.g., details about key decision-makers, budgets, timing, current technologies or buying processes). See Trade Show Math in Chapter 2.

** Pro Tip – Minimum Data Capture for Follow-Ups **

There are four things you need to capture:

- Name
- Company
- Contact information
- Something you will remember them by
  - Your conversation — e.g., Where they are from, something they said, accent
  - What they were wearing — e.g., Red shirt, fedora, cowboy boots

- Business cards
  - Yes, it is old school, but they are very effective. People digest your name and ask about your company upon receiving your card.
    - It is fast to share and there is a brief tactile component that solidifies memories.
      - They touch it, they read your name and company.
      - They know where you are from.
  - The recipient can write on it.
  - You can write on their card.
    - You can jot a quick note on it like "call me about ABC problem" or "introduce me to XYZ buyer."
  - Cards are becoming unique because everyone just connects on LinkedIn.
    - NOTE: You can put your LinkedIn link in a QR code on your card or you can add more details with some other apps.
  - It is easier to sort when the recipient gets home.

** Pro Tip – Business Cards **

Put your cards in your right pocket (outbox) and the cards you receive in your left pocket (inbox). The takeaway: keep them in different places for smooth delivery and reception.

- LinkedIn profile
  - LinkedIn is one of the best tools for events. Everyone always has a smartphone on their person today. If they are in business, they probably have a LinkedIn profile.
  - It is easy and fast to exchange information.
    - Press the Search area and a QR code will come up that they can scan to get your information.
    - If the app is not open already on your phone, you can press on the app and choose "Scan QR Code," tap on it and your profile is ready to scan with any camera on a phone.
- Credit card
  - For a variety of expenses from cabs to bar tabs
- Cash
  - For tipping your bartenders and servers
  - It is customary to tip in North America at industry functions

- Identification
  - License or other picture ID is important to get into licensed establishments in North America, regardless of age or if you have gray hair! I have seen 60-year-old men rejected at the door in the USA.
  - ID is also vital if your hotel key doesn't work, which can happen if it was stored too close to your phone or other credit cards.
- Hotel key
  - Obvious but this is a comprehensive list
- Phone or smartwatch
  - Nothing happens without a smartphone today ... it's probably attached to you.
  - Again, obvious but this is a comprehensive list

** Pro Tip – Personalize Follow-Ups from Your Notes **
  - After show, review all recent scans to create a follow-up list.
  - Message them directly on LinkedIn to stimulate next steps ... and yes, use the notes you took about them to personalize your messages.
- Show apps
  - Most shows now utilize a show app
    - Definition
      - An event-specific application that provides information about the show
        - Schedules
        - Sponsors
        - Contacts
        - FAQs

Chapter 9 – Extraverts, Introverts and Ambiverts – Who Are You?

Networking is not natural for most people, and there are different types of personalities that like, dislike or are neutral about networking. The reality is you need to practice and work at it.

Work is the operative word in NET-WORK. It is not net-play, net-eat, net-drink ... it is network!

> "Building a network doesn't have to be hard, but it does require intentional, focused work."
>
> Allison McWilliams, Ph.D.,
> Wake Forest University

Allison McWilliams'[35] article in "Psychology Today,"[36] "Why We Need Strong, Diverse Networks Now More Than Ever," points out that "Building a network doesn't have to be hard, but it does require intentional, focused work."

So put in the work. Intentional relationship-building is a game-changer. Let's get to work. Knowing who you are will help you to figure out what you need to work on to get started. There is no such thing as perfect networking — you practice networking. It may feel like you are out of your comfort zone. You can do it!

> "Move out of your comfort zone. You can only grow if you are willing to feel awkward and uncomfortable when you try something new."
>
> Brian Tracy

---

[35] Assistant VP of Mentoring and Alumni Personal and Career Development at Wake Forest University

[36] https://www.psychologytoday.com/intl/blog/your-awesome-career/202412/why-we-need-strong-diverse-networks-now-more-than-ever

Extraverts – Butterflies

Most people think extraverts are at the top of the food chain when it comes to networking because of their gregarious nature. It appears that way in a room, but there are things that they need to work on as well. Extraverts collect people and make rapid connections like butterflies going from flower to flower. In some cases, extraverts can be "relationship brokers."

- Description
    - Their encounters are usually quick and to the point, then they move on.
    - They tend to talk more than they listen, but can be a fantastic person at events, especially as part of a team.
    - They get more energized around people and recharge while they sleep.
- Things to work on:
    - Partner with an introvert.
    - Slow down, listen and build trust.
    - Take notes and capture information.
    - Schedule next steps and follow up.

Introverts – Icebergs

As a rule, introverts don't want to be the center of attention, which allows them to focus on the person they are talking to. They are naturally better listeners; therefore, they build trust and real long-term relationships. They tend to go deeper into a conversation. Like an iceberg, you only see a little bit of them until you get under the surface … or until they let you.

- Description
    - Introverts will connect more deeply with fewer people.
    - Their encounters tend to be longer and include deeper discussions.
    - They tend to listen more than they talk and can be both great individual networkers and/or part of a team that the extravert can hand people off to; let the extravert expend energy while the introvert relaxes.
    - They need quiet time to recharge; they need more breaks during the event.
- Things to work on:
    - Partner with an extravert or another introvert.
    - Set a goal to exceed the number of people that you met last time.
    - Schedule a lot of rest before and after events.
    - Be methodical and intentional with your interactions.

Ambivert – Zebra

An ambivert can be a networking animal, but which set of stripes will dominate will depend on the moment. They can lean either way in a conversation depending on who they are talking with and how they feel that day.

- Description
    - A personality style that lies somewhere between an introvert and an extravert
    - Depending on the day or who they interact with, they can show both extravert and introvert tendencies
- Things to work on:
    - Be aware of which way you are leaning early at an event and adjust accordingly
    - See extravert and introvert suggestions above, as mood may differ from day to day

** Pro Tip – Provide Introverts with Activities **

At a Boye & Co.[37] event in Europe, a puzzle was placed in a quieter zone of the networking space. These areas provided introverts with a "decompression zone" and it attracted some "birds of a feather" or other introverts. It also doubled as a reenergizing zone for introverts, who often find themselves exhausted after hours with large groups of people and extraverts.

"Introverts might enjoy doing a 1,000-piece puzzle in the middle of a conference because it offers a quiet, focused challenge amid the social buzz. The difficulty level is just right — hard enough to be engaging, but not overwhelming — giving them a satisfying struggle for their brains. It's an opportunity to recharge while still being present, allowing for moments of connection without the pressure of constant conversation. Plus, the slow, methodical process of fitting pieces together mirrors the way introverts often prefer to process information — thoughtfully and deeply."

Janus Boye — CEO, Boye & Co.

---

[37] Source: Boye conferences - Boye & Company - next-stage networking

Figure 29 – Puzzles for introverts

Energy – Refill Your Cup

What if I get tired? Congratulations, you are tired because you are working hard!

If a show is longer than two days, you will become tired regardless of which "vert" you are. If you are an introvert, you will be more tired than your extravert peers.

What can you do?

Sleep

- Know yourself. Sleep. If you need to sleep for eight hours per day, build your networking around that. For example, leave the networking function at 10:15 p.m. and wake up at 6:45 (yes, I provided time to get to your room and perform your sleep hygiene routine prior to going to bed).
- If you must decide between working out and late-night networking, go with the late-night networking. You will get more return on your time, as more people will attend the late-night events versus working out.
- DO attend breakfast!
  - Not only are these quieter networking times for introverts, but they are also usually quieter times on exhibit floors since show organizers will often incorporate breakfasts on show floors to drive traffic for exhibitors.

If you are an introvert, you energize by yourself. Use these tips to reenergize yourself alone:

- Take a session off and go for a walk outside or go to your room
- Take a nap
- Sit quietly by yourself
- Grab a coffee
- Take a book and read for 20 minutes
- Call home

Eat and hydrate

- Like an athlete, you need to keep your energy up. This comes from food and water.
- Yes, you can have an extra caffeinated beverage or a sugary snack, but be aware that it may affect your sleep, so be careful. Drink water, it's everywhere at an event.

Eat well and snack on the healthy snacks too.

Practice

They say to master something for 10,000 hours, so start today. This may be a playbook or a guide, but you must practice. You must run the drills and get the repetitions in. Practice active listening. Both shy and extraverted individuals alike benefit from actively listening during conversations.

Learn from Each Other

People often ask me, "How did you learn this stuff?"

It comes from years of observation, conversations, making mistakes and taking away lessons from others — both good and bad.

In a blog about taking his son to a conference[38], Matt Garrepy wrote that he observed his son, watching how he and others networked, and then he put his own spin on it. Networking basics exist, but over time you develop your own style or artistic impression like any professional.

> "Throughout the event, I noticed how keenly he (my son) was studying my tactics. He asked questions about our services and expressed genuine interest in learning more. Those queries allowed me to improve my own messaging, simplify things, and be a little more direct in my delivery.
>
> In this way, the student became the teacher."
>
> Matt Garrepy
> CMS Critic

---

[38] "I took my 20-year-old son on a business trip. Here's what I learned from him — and how it improved my work (and my rap skills)," LinkedIn

In a *From Pixels to Purpose* newsletter[39] by Karla Santi, she discussed how we eventually go from learning to leading. The article was entitled "Why Are People Taking Notes? Am I the Expert Now?"

> "We don't suddenly wake up feeling like we've 'arrived' at the perfect balance of wisdom and relevance. Instead, we grow into it, constantly shifting between learning and leading. And as we do, we realize that the real measure of experience isn't just how much we've accomplished but how much we're willing to share."
>
> Karla Santi
> CEO, Blend Interactive

People like Karla are out there at events on stage, NOW, but it took time to get there. They learned from others, appreciated the journey, and are still learning, but also giving back. These types of people are approachable. Yes, they are busy; yes, they may have big titles, but they are human and want to meet people too, to share and continue learning from you as well.

---

[39] https://www.linkedin.com/pulse/why-people-taking-notes-am-i-expert-now-karla-santi-49hkc/?trackingId=eu8wY0dgSAkk0GvBlfHLDA%3D%3D

Chapter 10 – Networking Mindset and Movements

All professionals start with the basics and then get more intricate or elaborate over time. Be strong on the basics, like any coach would say, and when in doubt, return to the basics. Here are some basics you need to work on. You can practice these by yourself, or you can simply prepare ahead of time by reviewing the following list.

Be Fearless

This is easier said than done, but again, it is a mindset. Yes, I still get a bit nervous entering a room of complete strangers. Remember, everyone is there for the same reasons as you: to network, learn and get a return on their investment.

In a blog post entitled "Networking: Conquering your fear[40]," Jason Noble suggests that understanding your fear is the first step to overcoming it. He states that three common types of fear hold us back:

1. Fear of rejection
2. Uncertainty
3. Social anxiety

"Remember, networking is a skill that can be improved over time.

By approaching it with a positive mindset, practicing active listening, setting realistic goals, and seeking support when needed, you can unlock the full potential of networking and pave the way for meaningful connections and opportunities."

Jason Noble
Chief Executive Officer, Noble Search Group Inc.

To overcome these obstacles, we both agree that there are some things that one can do to prepare and get in the right mindset. Many of these methods are addressed in the following sections of this book.

---

[40] https://www.linkedin.com/pulse/networking-conquering-your-fear-jason-noble-erfbc/

Rude People Exist

It does not matter who you are or how awesome you are, there are rude people on this planet. They may not always be rude or mean, but at the moment of interaction with you they might have been.

If someone is mean or rude, they don't deserve to talk to you.

If someone ignores you, they don't deserve to talk to you.

We are all equally important on this planet, we are just in different roles and places. You are at the event, you belong there. You may be absolutely ignorant about the subject, or you may have never been to an event in this market, but someone had the confidence in you, to send you to represent them.

Soak that in!!!

You may not be able to contribute groundbreaking "thought leadership" or ideas, but you should soak in the opportunity that you are now being exposed to.

To the rude, mean and snobby … treat both junior and senior people with the same respect. There was a time when you were at your first conference. Be nice and be welcoming.

Leaders: you need to provide opportunities to the up-and-comers and be willing to give your time to support them, whether that person is on your team or because they had the guts to approach you.

I thank all of those that believed in me and gave me a few extra moments of their time to build my confidence to overcome my imposter syndrome[41]. Some strategies you can use to overcome imposter syndrome[42]:

- Accept positive feedback.
- Break out of your comfort zone.
- Reframe your view of competence.
- Own your success.
- Reassess the gap between yourself and others.
- Stay mindful of your thoughts.

---

[41] Definition: The persistent inability to believe that one's success is deserved or has been legitimately achieved as a result of one's own efforts or skills. Source: https://www.oed.com/search/dictionary/?scope=Entries&q=impostor%20syndrome

[42] https://www.helpguide.org/mental-health/wellbeing/imposter-syndrome-causes-types-and-coping-tips

Act Like You Are the Host

Hosts know everyone, for the most part, because they have invited the guests to the event. So, you have to get into the mindset that you are the host, and all of these people are glad to be there to see you and everyone else. Once you get into that headspace there are a few tactical things you should practice.

- Introduce yourself and anyone else nearby you know to the person you just met.
- Say their name three times in the first two minutes, so you can remember it.
  - For example:
    - "Hi, my name is Paul, what is your name?"
      - "I am Jenny, nice to meet you."
    - "Great to meet you too, Jenny." — #1
    - "So, Jenny, where are you from?" — #2
      - "I am from New York, and I am with Company X."
    - "I love New York, Jenny, how long have you lived there?" — #3
  - Data capture
    - Name — Jenny (check out badge for last name, if it is not stated)
    - Company — Company X (confirm spelling on badge)
    - Contact information — Get that upon exit or use show app, or use LinkedIn if business cards or information is not shared
    - Something distinguishing about them — Red hair, short, lots of jewelry

Set a Goal

You can set a variety of goals, such as the number of people you want to meet or a set list of people you want to meet. Just start with something manageable. As you become more comfortable, raise your goals like you would add weights to your barbells in the gym.

Entering and Exiting Conversations

This is probably one of the hardest aspects of networking. It can be uncomfortable on both ends of the conversation, but it is critical to your time management and to ensure that you are maximizing your networking time.

How and when do you enter a conversation?

How do you avoid being rude?

Here are a few socially accepted principles that apply. They are not 100% perfect but they are very good guidelines.

Entering Conversations

Use the LALA method to engage with people in the room. LALA is an acronym for Look, Access, Listen and Approach. This method allows you to slowly get rolling in a polite and noninvasive way.

- Look — Start by reading the crowd
- Access — Pick a spot to get started
- Listen — For an opportunity to get in
- Approach — Join in

Let's dive deeper into this methodology.

Reading the Crowd – Who is Open to Conversation?

Nobody likes to be startled or feel "under attack" by an overenthusiastic networker. We're not out to hunt for our next meal like a wild animal. We're out to meet people, learn and hopefully expand our network of people we can help or who can help us in the future. So, reading the crowd's body language is critical. You need to observe who is physically open to conversation. Once you find an "open to conversation" opportunity, you pick your access point and listen for an opportunity to enter the conversation. If there is a group, you can pick a lull in the conversation to enter. You can also make eye contact with one of the people in the conversation, and they may invite you in — approach them. If the person is by themselves, you can approach once you make eye contact with them, so you are not intimidating.

Proxemics

In an article titled "Establishing Rapport"[43] in "Science Direct," Robert E. Rakel shares an excerpt from the "Textbook of Family Medicine (Eighth Edition)," 2012, on the importance of proxemics — the study of how people unconsciously structure the space around them. He states that "This structuring varies with every culture. North Americans, for example, maintain a protective 'body bubble' of space about 2 feet in diameter around them when they interact with strangers or casual acquaintances. Violators of that space are considered intruders and cause the person to become defensive."

The concept of proxemics is a term introduced by anthropologist Edward T. Hall in 1966[44]. Proxemics studies how people perceive and use space in various contexts, particularly in North American cultures. Hall identified four distinct zones of interpersonal distance:

- Intimate space: Close physical contact up to 18 inches of space, typically shared between people in an intimate relationship
- Personal space: Between 18 inches and 4 feet, depending on whether you're speaking to a stranger, casual acquaintance, or close friend
- Social space: 4-12 feet of space provided in social settings, like a shared office space, or the distance between a presenter and their audience
- Public space: 12 feet or more, typically observed in shopping malls and airports

The net: You should be between 2 and 6 feet from people when interacting with them. Follow their lead and, of course, ensure you are comfortable as well.

---

[43] https://www.sciencedirect.com/topics/nursing-and-health-professions/proxemics
[44] *The Hidden Dimension*, Hall, Edward T.

Open to Conversation

There are physical indicators that a person is open to a conversation. They are actually "open." What do I mean by "open"? There are two scenarios: they are by themselves, or they are with two or more people in the shape of an arc or an open circle. See Figure 30 – Open to conversation.

Open Conversations

When a person or a group is open, you can enter that conversation by entering the open circle. In most cases, someone will invite you in by introducing themselves, or you can introduce yourself if they are quiet. If it is just one person, it is a simple one-on-one conversation. If it is a group, they have previously met. The group may have just met or may have known each other for a longer period of time. Either way they are physically receptive to someone entering their space. It is rare that you will be rejected, but there are some rude people on this planet.

Figure 30 – Open to conversation

Closed Conversations

If the two people are face to face, they are closed. If more than two people are in a circle, they are closed. See Figure 31 – Closed to conversations. Do not enter the circle or the conversation unless these people are well-known to you.

Figure 31 – Closed to conversations

Move on to find open circles or individuals.

Remember, if you form a conversation, keep it open, unless you are diving deeper into a conversation or subject matter that you want to remain private.

Exiting Conversations

Exiting conversations can be tough if you have been in one for a while or if the subject matter is going off on a random tangent. Excusing yourself gracefully is a necessary skill. If you need to move on, politely excuse yourself with one of the following methods.

- Simply say, "I'm off to meet some other people that I promised I would say hi to."
- You can say, "I'm going to get some food or another beverage."
- You can say hi to someone else you met earlier if they walk by.
- You can say, "I have to take this call," or "I have to respond to this text from my boss [or home]."

Explicit but polite version for the person that doesn't want to let you go:

- "It's been great talking with you. I'd love to continue this conversation later, but I want to make sure I meet a few more people."

Worst case — you can excuse yourself and go to the restroom/washroom.

Conversation Topics – What Do I Say When I Meet Strangers?

Here are some quick and easy conversation starters to keep in your arsenal. Make a copy of these and study them. You don't have to memorize them, but if you read them out loud and review them before you step out of your room, they will roll off your tongue with confidence and stimulate conversation.

Remember the old adage: "We have two ears and one mouth so that we can listen twice as much as we speak."[45]

- Basic topics
  - Why did you come to the show?
  - What company are you with?
    - What do you do for them?
  - How did you get into the business?
  - Where are you from?
    - Heritage — parents/grandparents
    - Location — city, state/province, country
- Fun topics
  - What would you be doing if you could do anything?
  - What book are you reading right now?
  - What do you do for fun?
- Segue[46]
  - I am a big fan of expanding on what others have said or asking more questions about the subject.
  - It is great to relate the topic to something in your life without detracting from the original story; be additive, not a one-upper.

Below are more icebreaker questions, because people are always asking me, "What do I say?"

Remember, most people enjoy talking about themselves because self-disclosure releases feel-good hormones.

- Where did you grow up?
- What did you do over the weekend?
- Did you do anything interesting over the holidays?
- What's your favorite hobby?
- What's your favorite thing about your work week?

---

[45] This quote is attributed to Epictetus, a Greek philosopher, circa 60 AD.
[46] Italian, literally "follows," or "to transition without interruption"

- How did you get into this line of work?
- What's your favorite part of your job?
- What cool things have you accomplished in the past year?
- How do you like to start your day?
- What projects have you been working on lately?
- What did you do for a summer job?
- Do you have any pets?
- What kind of music do you listen to?
- What's the best project you've worked on?
- Are you a sports fan?
- Are you a morning person or a night owl?
- What's your ideal holiday destination?
- What's your favorite food?
- What's your favorite place in the world?
- What are your favorite TV shows or movies?

Another way to come up with personalized questions or information to share with others during a networking moment is the "Personal User Manual," a concept that was first introduced by Ivar Kroghrud, the lead strategist at QuestBack. In a 2013 interview with Adam Bryant for the "New York Times" column "The Corner Office," Kroghrud discussed how he created a manual to help his colleagues understand his working style, preferences and expectations, aiming to enhance team collaboration and communication[47].

Today, many organizations encourage employees to create their own user manuals to foster better understanding, improve communication, and build psychological safety within teams.

Recently, I saw this "create your own user manual" concept documented by Matcha[48], a community matching platform that supports 1:1 introduction programs. This was part of a four-part blog entitled "30 Tips from Experts on How to Network and Connect With Authenticity." They stated that "Networking often starts by helping others. However, an equally important foundation of great connection is knowing yourself well, too. That's where creating a 'User Manual' comes in handy."[49]

Prepared questions are one way to prepare for networking opportunities; however, a lady I met through an online networking group is a big proponent of improvisation.

---

[47] "A personal user manual for working with me," Friday.app

[48] https://matcha.so/

[49] https://matcha.so/blog/how-to-network-and-connect-with-authenticity-3

This disrupts the preparation process I describe above but this too can be learned and practiced.

> "Networking is about human connection and building authentic relationships by showing up as your true self. Applied improvisation, with its focus on curiosity, openness, and active listening, helps us create meaningful connections through the 'Yes, And' mindset."
>
> Tracy Shea-Porter
> CEO and co-founder, Yes Unlimited

Tracy Shea-Porter, CEO and co-founder of Yes Unlimited, wrote a book on the subject — *The "Yes, And" Business Evolution: Improv Skills for Leadership and Life*.[50] She believes that active listening and remaining curious can both enrich conversations and deepen connections.

Regardless of how you prepare, it is important to get in the right place mentally.

** Pro Tip – Get in the Right Mindset **

Many of our most popular communication inventions (e.g., phone, FaceTime, text messaging, video conferencing) have been to simulate a face-to-face discussion, so maximize it!

- Act like a host.
- Be fearless — you deserve to be in the room.
- Set a personal goal.
- Be rested going into the event.
- Stay hydrated.
    - If you consume alcohol, have at least one glass of water for every 1-2 drinks.
- Write notes; you will have information overload.
    - Consolidate the themes or patterns from the show on the plane ride home or your first week back in the office.
- Have fun and improvise a bit!

---

[50] A book about applied improvisation, the rising "Yes, And" approach conceived from comedy improv to enhance team building and leadership skills through experiential training.

Chapter 11 – Last Call

Disclaimer

Before we get deeper into this subject, it is very important to state that this section is not implying that you should be drinking alcohol all night or at all.

In fact, you should not drink alcohol all night. You should hydrate with water. At the very least, you should drink water between alcoholic and caffeinated beverages to remain hydrated and in control.

In this book, "last call" is a generic moment in time that implies you are networking up to the last possible available time to network. Of course, the actual time depends on the facility and your personal endurance. However, maximizing this time can enrich the development of relationships.

See Levels of Networking Events.

Here are a few practical tips and thoughts about how to execute this properly.

Dress Code

What do I wear? What do I pack?

Know the schedule and the events. There might be some themes, or it may be a more reserved crowd. Here are some general tips.

- Dress appropriately.
- Dress above what you believe the average will be.
    - Business casual is always safe but be prepared for more.
- Wear comfortable shoes.
    - Bring two different pairs and alternate for comfort as you will be on your feet a lot.

** Pro Tip – Memorable Outfits **
- Wear a signature outfit if you are that type of person ... be you!
    - If there is a theme:
        - Hawaiian shirt
        - Favorite sports team shirt
    - Unique outfits or accessories:
        - Leather jacket
        - Bow ties / colorful ties
        - Top hats / fedoras

You Are in the Mixer or Event ... Now What?

You have set your goals.

You are armed with your tools.

You have studied how to approach people.

It is time to put these strategies into practice. LALA, discussed earlier, works in open spaces well, but what if it is a little busier?

There are not a lot of rules but there are a few methods you can try, especially if you are starting out by yourself or with a small group. My favorite is the beachfront property method.

The "Beachfront Property" Method

This is my personal favorite maneuver at a bar. It is fun and, more importantly, it works!

What is it?

It is the creation of a literal, physical sales "funnel" of opportunities that walk right into you, through a funnel of space or humans.

You enact this maneuver by sitting at a prime spot at a bar (aka the beachfront property) by yourself, with a colleague or industry acquaintance. Essentially, there are two to three seats between a person who wants a beverage and the bartender. This person has walked right onto "your beach," the space you have locked up because you have established position or ownership of your piece of valuable "beachfront." You are physically between the prospects and the bar. They must go through you or around you to order a drink.

Figure 32 – The path to the beachfront property

At peak times, the bartenders are busy and in demand. If you have the established position and your own "personal" bartender (one you have met prior to someone approaching your beach), you are in control of the flow of drinks.

Setting Up the Funnel

Timing

- You should show up and establish position after the estimated average dinnertime. If you are solo, show up and eat at the bar if they have a dinner menu, to ensure your position.
- Keep in mind that your position can be established at the busiest bar at the mixer or in a hotel bar, or even an event social.
- The key is to get into position and hold it.

The People

- Solo — one person
- Partner — two people
- Team — three to five people — a diverse team is most effective
  - Man
  - Woman
  - Person of color
  - Customer
  - Vendor
- Note: A big, main character type can be both good and bad
  - They attract a lot of attention, which can attract some people but turn off others.

The Place

- A seat or two or three at the center of the bar

Beverage Budget

- Start a tab but know the upper end of the budget.

A Primary and Secondary Bartender

- Befriend and tip a bartender early and well.
- A secondary bartender and/or the manager are also good people to know ahead of time.

Now that the funnel is built, the prospects or new unknown people will begin to enter.

B = Bartender

K = Known person or networking partner

? = Unknown person or prospective new acquaintances

Figure 33 – Prospect entering the beachfront

127

** Pro Tip – Beachfront Property Steps **

- When someone wants to order a drink, you do the following:
  - Make a little room for them to get close enough to order the drink.
  - If the bartender is not paying attention, call them by name.
  - When the person has ordered or is waiting to order their drink:
    - Ask if they are with your event.
    - If they are, introduce yourself and your supporting cast if you have people with you.
    - Ask them what firm they are with and what they do.
    - If they are a prospective customer, put the drink on your tab when they try to pay.
    - Exchange information:
      - Business card
      - LinkedIn profile
  - When they get their drink, they will thank you.
    - Write down their information and look them up on the show app if you have time.
  - Repeat.
  - Take note of fun people and make a mental note of six to ten people with whom you would like to take your networking to the next level ... see below.

Levels of Networking Events

Levels 1 and 2, below, will be organized or happen organically. However, Levels 3 to 5 take work to organize or to encourage others to participate in.

- Level 1 — The organized happy hour on show floor or near it
- Level 2 — The sponsored or informal dinners
- Level 3 — The post-dinner sponsored or informal events
- Level 4 — The hotel bar
- Level 5 — The after-party — usually off campus

Levels 3 to 5 are where deeper conversations can happen, and the bonding or relationships solidify. Stories and how people "remember the way you make them feel" are galvanized in these areas. "Inside baseball" or undocumented information about prospects, such as upcoming changes at organizations, from role changes to new hires or even additional investments, are often heard here.

Level 1 Notes

Level 1 is the easiest level.

Show up at all organized events, happy hours or breaks. This is the absolute minimum you should do.

Level 2 Notes

Although for the most part you will be able to find someone to dine with, or if you are a prospect, you will probably be invited to a dinner party, it is possible you may be left out. If you are an introvert or have dietary restrictions, you could use this time as a recharge time or to eat what you want.

However, if you are networking hard, you should try to find a group of people to dine with. It could be a formal partner or customer dinner or a sponsored dinner by one of the large vendors. They will usually invite you weeks in advance as they may have a finite number of seats to fill. As the dinners get closer, though, last-minute decisions are made and seats become available, so do not think that every dinner is "sold out."

"Crashing" dinners or events is sometimes welcomed because they are already paid for, and they want to maximize their event investment. Marketing is trying to maximize their attributable leads, and the company wants to increase their chances of winning new business. See Crashing Parties and Social Events below.

** Pro Tip – Buffet Dinners Are Easier to Crash **

The food is paid for, and in some cases "the more, the merrier" applies.

Crashing Parties and Social Events

This is an important idea for networking in general, but this skill may also be helpful to support you in networking at Levels 3-5.

There are usually two to three marquee events at a conference. You need to find out where these clandestine events are and who has the power to get you on the list or into the event if you are not invited.

There are several ways into an event. Here are a few strategies.

- Customers are always powerful. Everyone wants customers and prospects at their events to maximize their ROI or to reduce their payback period. It's important to get to know prospects and customers, and where they are going, during earlier networking opportunities. If a prospect befriends you and has the power to "bring a friend," their vendor will not refuse you entry. Refusing would make them look bad in front of their prospect or customer.
- Partners are also known by the host and are like customers because they do business together. Asking partners where they are going can guide your decisions and point you in the right direction. Partners want to grow their relationships with their business partners, and they want to earn new business as well.
- Well-known people in the industry or even the people that work at the event also know which strings to pull. They know what is happening outside of the organized networking events as well. They all want to be where the biggest crowds are. The biggest crowds are the largest marketplace of the moment.

Suppose you know where the venue is, but you don't have a way in?

Show up ... you have nothing to lose!

You are starting from zero, and the worst thing that can happen is that you are not allowed in right away or at the peak time of entry. As the event goes on, people will leave because they may have more than one place to be. Others may not even show up because they overcommitted to too many events. Look for a table full of unused badges (i.e., not picked up).

As Harvey Mackay once wrote, "There is no such thing as a sold-out house."[51]

---

[51] Mackay, Harvey. *Swim with the Sharks Without Being Eaten Alive: Outsell, Outmanage, Outmotivate, and Outnegotiate Your Competition.* William Morrow, 1988.

Others you have met throughout the conference may arrive and take you in with them. They may "know a guy" or know the person who is policing the door. So be patient, be observant, be friendly and talk to others.

Level 3 Notes

Level 3 is similar to Level 2 but is focused on the events that may take place shortly after dinnertime, and locations may or may not be known beforehand. It may be on a chartered boat, at a rooftop bar, or at a bowling alley. So, once again, do your homework early; you may have to sign up. See Figure 34 – Application or sign-up for VIP event. You may know a few folks that are "in the know," such as vendors or partners, and from there you can execute to the best of your ability.

Have fun, make a new friend and be the real you.

You are now at the level where it is quality over quantity. One conversation is good enough here.

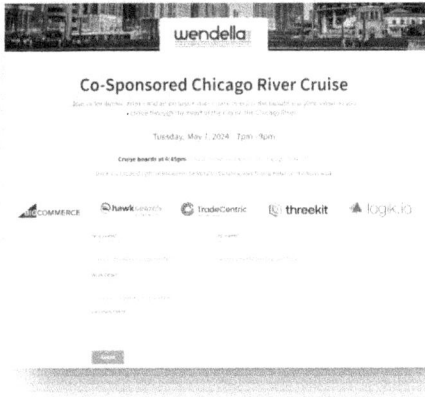

Figure 34 – Application or sign-up for VIP event

** Pro Tip – Have Something to Give or Know What You Want to Get **

This is the exception to the "networking is not transactional" rule.

Specific and valuable information exchange can be an incentive for someone to extend their day, as it's worth it for them to learn something of significance. The aim could be to finish a conversation or start a conversation about something you could not really get into earlier because too many people were around. So, before you get to this level, know who you want to spend a few valuable moments with. Refer to your notes and add these people to your goal.

In 2015, I had the opportunity to meet Maureen Goodson, the executive director of National Postal Forum (NPF) at the time, at a function sponsored by a current partner of my company at the time, BCC Software. Shawn Ryan and Mitch Carpenter, industry event veterans and Level 3 comrades of mine from past events, invited me to participate in their event. They mentioned that it would be well attended, with guests including their president Chris Lien and some influential people in the industry. As we were socializing, the gentlemen from BCC introduced me to a variety of people.

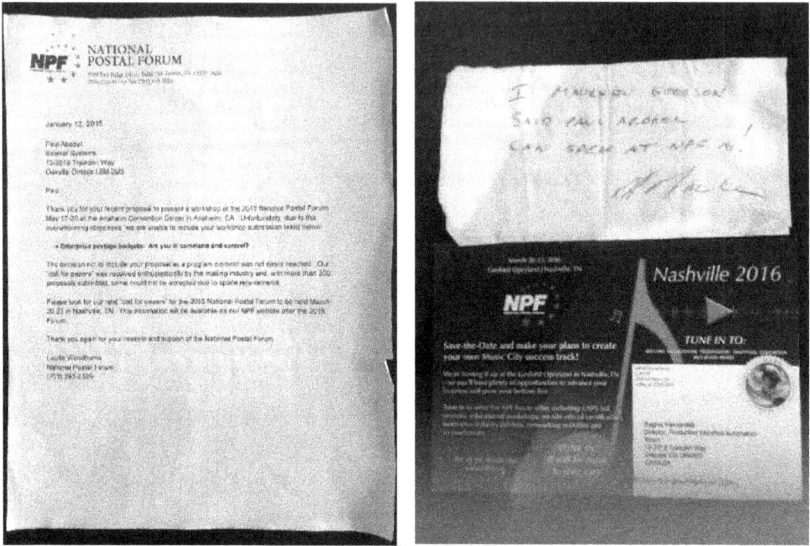

Figure 35 – Napkin contract

A few weeks prior to the 2015 conference, I had received a kind and diplomatic speaker rejection letter from NPF. I was disappointed and felt that my topic warranted a spot. In addition, I also noticed while at the show that there were several well-known industry consultants with three to five speaking slots each. When I was introduced to the lovely lady that sent me the well-worded rejection letter, I decided to ask, "What are you looking for in a good speaker?" I then went on to state somewhat sarcastically, "Do I need to know someone to get into the lineup?"

She introduced me to Maureen, who was standing a few feet from us. When Maureen heard my story, she asked me what my subject was, and I told her. She said, "We could have used that subject this year. I will include you in next year's speaker lineup." I said, "Can I get that in writing?" I found a napkin (Figure 35 – Napkin contract) and created a fun contract. She signed it on the spot, and I used the napkin with my speaker submission for the 2016 conference. My submission was accepted, and it kick-started a flurry of positive activity.

This was the beginning of my being recognized as a subject matter expert in the industry. That moment led to being on two boards, including the US Postmaster General's Mailers Technical Advisory Committee (MTAC). As of the writing of this book, I believe I am still the only Canadian/non-American to serve on that committee.

Level 4 Notes

There can be attrition when people are tired or spread out across multiple dinners or events. However, the hotel bar provides a moment for everyone to take a deep breath as they wind down their day — their last call. People gravitate to it for networking moments before, during and after events. In some cases, it may be a place for colleagues to debrief or for others with multiple commitments that day to gather.

Like ancient "central business districts," this accessible location for social and commercial gatherings is easy. Encouraging people with no plans to hang out there can allow you to create your own mini-event and establish your beachfront property early in the night.

If you are out at another event, getting folks to stay for another 30-60 minutes may not always be easy, but it is easier if you are at the host hotel.

If you have not been able to connect with someone you have wanted to talk to, this is usually an easy place to find them. Be forewarned that this is a bonus level. There could be some informal prearranged meetings that may exclude you; don't be offended, and read the room.

If you do strike up a conversation with someone you know (partner, prospect or customer), this time solidifies relationships and trust. People are usually in search of "the truth" and the stories that are not published. They may ask harder hitting questions like what the true total cost of ownership is, the real implementation timelines or the actual level of difficulty of achieving results and impact.

Figure 36 – The hotel bar

** Pro Tip – Order a Round of Waters **

Everyone has been out for a while, and if they have had a drink or three, they will welcome a round of waters. Grab a pitcher of water from the bartender that you have befriended and a few glasses. This will also demonstrate some maturity and a level of responsibility. Refill that pitcher once or twice and refill their glasses.

The time on the clock is between 10:00 p.m. and 11:30 p.m.
This is a great exit point.

You are most likely in or near your hotel and an elevator ride away from your room.

Level 5 Notes

The after-party can be a valuable but a very chaotic and challenging level. People are tired and may have had more drinks than usual. They are becoming like a room of cats to herd. They may also be in several locations, so this is not easy to execute.

Figure 37 – The after-party

You have two choices at this fork in the road:

1. Leave and prepare for the next day.
    a. Probably the best choice to stay fresh and re-energize for the following day.
    b. This will prevent you from making ill-advised decisions like spending too much money, engaging in too many drinks or simply getting lost in an unfamiliar city.
2. Engage at your own risk.
    a. If you do engage, there are pros and cons.
    b. Read on below.

** Pro Tip – Build Your Own Team **

This is a group of fun people you trust, but they should also be effective networkers.

- Why fun people?
  - If they are not fun or "magnetic," others will not follow.
- Trust is important: this group will have your back and keep you safe.
- They may be influential in the community.
  - Senior executives
  - Speakers
  - Analysts
  - Community founders
  - Board members

Micro-groups

- Definition: a small group of people that are already connected to each other
- Consolidating two to five micro-groups into a "macro-group" can create momentum and the energy required to ignite level 5

Logistics and Preparation

Like any good movement or team, communication and organization are critical to keeping everyone together and containing the "herd of cats." By gathering contact information of the micro-group leaders throughout the event and evening, you can be the central point of contact for the macro-group. Creating a WhatsApp group of the micro-group leaders, or a group chat in whatever social media you use, will facilitate smooth execution.

Please note that you do not have to be the organizer, but you need to be part of a micro-group to know what is happening at this point.

How can you tell who the micro-group leaders are?

Simple ... they usually have a few colleagues with them or a group of friends, partners or customers from prior events. They are usually a "main character" personality or somewhat of an extravert. They usually have a group around them. They may also be part of large groups at Level 1 events.

Research Close and Fun Local Places

This is an underrated skill and of utmost importance. This needs to be done earlier in the day, not on the fly. It needs to be orchestrated and methodically messaged to your team.

- Universal fun places in walking distance or short car rides (under five minutes):
    - Karaoke bars
    - Bars with live bands
    - Duelling piano bars
    - Pool halls

Why pre-planned locations?

When people are having fun and the environment becomes noisy and buzzing, organizing people becomes very difficult. Especially if they are people of power and influence.

The leaders take two forms:

1. They always want to be in charge because they are used to overseeing everything, or
2. They want a break from organizing and appreciate being led.

These experiences will become the folklore that will solidify your position in the "industry club."

I guarantee that these events will help you to form long-term friendships and potential business relationships, if you are under control and you have fun.

Remember ... this is net-work, not net-drink.

Drink responsibly and be professional.

Leave nobody behind, and if things get out of hand, leave in a taxi or rideshare!

Post-Show

Make networking a biweekly habit ... as in twice per week.

I use the Tuesday/Thursday Trigger Timeslot (4Ts) methodology for reaching out to people I have not spoken to in a while. A while could be two months or two years.

Every Tuesday and Thursday morning from 8:00-8:15 a.m. I have a calendar item to reach out to someone to give them a "free hello" or to book a meeting with them in the near future. A free hello is when you call someone or book a meeting with someone with no transaction in mind. You are simply enriching your relationship.

Form the habit — you don't have to be perfect — and try to be consistent. This proactive behavior will pay for itself over time. You might not get a deal tomorrow or this quarter, but you are building a diversified, lifelong pipeline of trust that can pay dividends at some point in time.

I know, I know, you get busy with work and then your networking may suffer. If you don't put water and sunshine on a plant, it dies. It is not as extreme with a person in your network, but it is similar.

Earn trust over time ... and network *From Workout to Last Call*.

Appendices

All of the worksheets can be accessed using this QR code to go to paulabdool.ca.

Appendix A – Business Cases

Trade Show Business Case

Trade show business cases should include all of your costs and an estimated return on event. The high-level components are below.

Conference details:

- Name of conference:

- Date(s) of conference:

- Location:

- Expected number of attendees:

Expenses:

1. Exhibitor fees:

    - Booth rental:

    - Additional booth services (electricity, internet, etc.):

    - Marketing:

        - Promotional items printing (flyers, brochures, banners):

        - Advertising (online, print, social media):

        - Website development/management:

2. Registration fees for brand ambassadors:

    - For additional brand ambassadors not included in your exhibitor fees

    - Note if there are early bird registrations or late registration fees

        - This will stimulate prompt decision-making

3. Sponsorship opportunities/fees:

    - Gold Sponsor, Silver Sponsor, Bronze Sponsor, etc.

- Ensure you maximize your sponsorship benefits or even ask for more to build your business case (e.g., a speaking opportunity, prominent booth position)

4. Marketing and promotion:

5. Brand ambassadors:

- Travel expenses, meals:

Total expenses:

Note: Expenses can be divided or shared by partners. This strengthens business cases, value propositions and partnerships.

Estimated income:

1. Forecasted deals

- Decision-makers that will be in attendance with active committed deals in the pipeline

- Decision-makers that will be in attendance with active strong upside deals in the pipeline

- Note: Whatever forecasting metrics your firm uses should be used here

2. Current customers

- Customers that are in the "renewal sales cycle"

- Customers that are prospects for upsell and cross-sell opportunities

- Customers that are at risk of churn

3. Partners

- Current partners that are co-selling prospects

Total estimated income:

Net income (or loss) (income - expenses):

Notes/comments:

Additional details, explanations or comments regarding specific line items or overall budget should be part of a business case.

Attendee Business Case

Attending industry conferences can significantly benefit both individuals and the organizations they represent. Here are several key justifications for attending:

1. **Networking opportunities:** Conferences provide unparalleled networking opportunities, allowing attendees to connect with industry peers, potential clients, partners, and experts. Building and nurturing professional relationships can lead to new business opportunities, collaborations and valuable insights.

2. **Knowledge sharing and learning:** Conferences feature sessions, workshops and keynote presentations delivered by industry leaders and experts. These sessions cover the latest trends, best practices, case studies, and innovations in the field, offering attendees valuable knowledge and skills that they can apply in their work.

3. **Staying updated on industry trends:** Industries are constantly evolving, with new technologies, regulations and market trends emerging regularly. Conferences offer a comprehensive overview of the current state of the industry, including emerging trends, market disruptions and future projections. Staying updated on industry trends is essential for professionals to remain competitive and relevant in their field.

4. **Professional development:** Conferences often offer opportunities for professional development, such as certifications, training courses and skill-building workshops. These programs can help attendees enhance their skills, expand their knowledge base and advance their careers.

5. **Market intelligence and insights:** Conferences provide a platform for industry leaders to share market intelligence, insights and strategic perspectives. By attending conference sessions and engaging in discussions with peers and experts, attendees gain valuable insights into market dynamics, competitive landscape, customer preferences, and growth opportunities.

6. **Brand visibility and reputation:** Attending industry conferences can enhance an individual's or organization's brand visibility and reputation within the industry. Active participation, such as speaking engagements, panel discussions, or sponsoring events, can increase visibility and

position the attendee or organization as a thought leader and influencer in the industry.

7. **Lead generation and business development:** Conferences offer opportunities for lead generation and business development through networking, exhibition booths and sponsored events. Engaging with potential clients, partners and collaborators at conferences can lead to new business opportunities, partnerships and collaborations.

8. **Motivation and inspiration:** Conferences provide a motivational and inspirational environment, where professionals can interact with like-minded individuals, celebrate successes and gain motivation to overcome challenges and pursue their goals. The energy and enthusiasm of fellow attendees can be contagious and rejuvenating.

Email Template to Manager

Subject: Request to attend [conference name]

Hi [manager's name],

I have researched this event and would like your approval to attend [conference name], which is scheduled to take place on [dates] in [location]. I believe attending this conference will provide numerous benefits not only for my professional growth but also for our team and the organization.

This conference will provide the following for both [your company name] and me: *(choose three to four significant reasons from the list below)*.

1. **Project research**
   The event will expedite my research to support project [name of current project] to ensure quality decision-making.

2. **Market intelligence and insights**
   Attending will provide valuable insights into market dynamics, customer preferences and growth opportunities. This knowledge can inform our strategies and decision-making processes.

3. **Staying updated on industry trends**
   With industries rapidly evolving, this conference offers a comprehensive overview of emerging technologies, market dynamics and future trends, ensuring we stay ahead of the curve and maintain our competitive edge.

4. **Professional development**
   The event includes workshops and training sessions that could enhance my skill set and broaden my knowledge base, which I can apply to my role and share with the team.

5. **Motivation and inspiration**
   Being part of such an energetic and innovative environment will provide fresh perspectives and inspiration that I can bring back to the team to help drive our collective success.

6. **Knowledge sharing and learning**
   The conference features sessions led by industry leaders covering the latest trends, best practices and innovations. I look forward to bringing back actionable insights that we can incorporate into our strategies.

7. **Networking opportunities**
   The event will provide an excellent chance to connect with industry peers, potential clients, partners and thought leaders. These connections could lead to new collaborations, insights and business opportunities that align with our objectives.

8. **Lead generation and business development**
   The networking and exhibition opportunities at the conference can help generate leads, identify potential partners, and open avenues for collaboration to support our goals.

The estimated cost of attending, including registration, travel and accommodations, is [estimated total]. Currently I have $ [insert any professional development budget you have here that can be used to offset or cover the costs if your organization has a program] in my professional development budget.

The most economical early bird registration ends by [mm/dd/yyyy], so it would be good to register prior to that.

Please let me know if you'd like to discuss this further or need additional information. I'd be happy to provide more details about the agenda and potential benefits.

Thank you for considering my request. I look forward to your thoughts.

Best regards,
[your name]

Note:

- Use the detailed budget estimate provided below if necessary. However, most managers just want to know the bottom line and if it will interfere with your current workload.
- If you can provide any value.

Attendee Budget Estimates

1. **Registration fees:**

    - Conference registration: $
    - Additional workshops/sessions: $
    - Networking events: $

2. **Travel expenses:**

    - Airfare/train/bus tickets: $
    - Transportation to/from airport/station: $
    - Local transportation (e.g., taxi, rideshare): $
    - Parking fees: $

3. **Accommodation:**

    - Hotel accommodation (number of nights x nightly rate): $

4. **Meals:**

    - Daily meals (number of days x estimated meal cost): $
    - Dinners/networking events: $

5. **Miscellaneous:**

    - Currency conversion fees: $

Total estimated cost: $

Appendix B – Return on Investment Worksheet

The Return on Investment worksheet should be simple. It can be an additional stand-alone worksheet, or it can be a worksheet within your master Annual Event Budget Planner.

I like it to feed into the Annual Event Planner to ensure that everything is in one place, since the overall budget of each event is already established within it and actual total spend is also captured in it.

Things to keep in mind:

- Minimum breakeven is within six months of your average sales cycle.
- Know the number of deals required to break even prior to attending.
- Include new logos, cross-sells and upsells that are attributable to the event.

It is worth repeating that trade show math is a bit messy, and attribution is also messy. It is rare that the event itself brings in business. However, all of the pre-event and post-event activities can support the live interactions. The live interactions and the relationship building at events can and will support the pipeline creation and the closing of new business.

Appendix C – Payback Period Worksheet

Unlike the Return on Investment worksheet, the Payback Period worksheet should be a separate metric. It may be informed by your CRM or by marketing to ensure that the event was worth it. It can also be a column in your master Annual Event Budget Planner.

I like it to feed into the Annual Event Planner to ensure that everything is in one place, since the overall budget of each event is already established within it and actual total spend is also captured in it.

Things to keep in mind:

- Minimum breakeven is within six months of your average sales cycle.
- Know the number of deals required to break even.
- Track the deals monthly at minimum and keep refreshing this worksheet.
- Attribution may be divided or split between marketing, sales, and partnership teams.
  - The perfect case scenario is that these three areas within a Go to Market (GTM) team should all be working together and winning together. Fighting over attribution is a waste of time and can create a toxic environment.

Appendix D – Annual Event Budget Template and Planner

An annual event budget is not easy to come up with. I have worked with a few great marketing and finance folks that used elaborate spreadsheets to keep everything in line. From financials to people management, it is critical to stay organized and to plan well ahead (i.e., Q3 of the preceding fiscal year).

This planner should be a "living document" to ensure that it is updated monthly or quarterly. This will inform future planning and provide a macro view to balance financial goals and brand ambassador burnout.

Here are some sample headings to consider:

- Event Name
- Brand Ambassadors
- Role
- Location
- Event Region
- Event Date
- Calendar Months (JAN, FEB, MAR, etc.)
- Q1
- Q2
- Q3
- Q4
- Event Budgets
- Approved Internally
- Event Contracts Signed
- Total Annual Event Budget
- Total Actual Spend
- Total Event Count
- Return on Event
- Payback Period
- Notes

Note: Actual expenses may vary depending on factors such as location, duration of stay, personal preferences and any additional activities planned during the trip. It's advisable to research and plan for expenses in advance to ensure a smooth and budget-conscious conference experience.

Appendix E – Event Budget Worksheet

Components of this Event Budget Worksheet could be stand-alone but can also be incorporated into the Annual Event Budget Worksheet. If you are just starting out and you have been given a rough budget for one or two events, you would probably start with something like this prior to building out the Annual Event Budget Worksheet.

Show overview

- Show name
- Dates
- Location
- City
- State
- Country

Meetings booked prior to the event

These are meetings and/or demonstrations that you expect to conduct at the event.

- Prospects
  - 1
  - 2
  - 3
  - Top 5 suspects/prospects post-show
- Customers
  - 1
  - 2
  - 3
- Partners
  - 1
  - 2
  - 3

Key metrics

Leads

- Number of leads generated from event

Meetings (actuals)

- Meetings with prospective customers

- Meetings with existing customers
- Meetings with existing partners
- Meetings with prospective partners
- Meetings booked after follow-up calls

Demos conducted

- Number/companies

Brand impressions

- Booth walk-bys / impressions
- Sponsorship impressions
- Social media impressions

Revenue and forecast

- Attributable revenue within six months (directly from event)
- Attributable opportunities within two months of event
- Partners' logos acquired within two months of event

ROI model

- Total cost of event
- Average cost per lead
- Average cost per impression

Actual ROI

- Total cost of event
- Actual sales — within six months of event

Appendix F – Badge Positioning and Etiquette

Shorten your lanyard!

Like clothes off the rack, lanyards need tailoring.

Why?

Eye contact

It positions your badge in the middle of your chest versus your belly button and makes it easier for others to read, while pretending to maintain eye contact, if they have forgotten your name. In Figure 38 – Badge positioning with Lancey Lexima, you can see that we are about the same height, but our badges are positioned differently. Mine makes it easier for people to read without moving their eyes too far from my face.

Incidentally, I met Lancey at a keynote address over breakfast (networking moment) because I sat at his table. Coincidentally, he worked at one of my company's partner firms at the time. I suggested we take a picture together to share with someone else at his company that I was working with. Someone at our table offered to take a picture with us, and they became part of my network too.

Figure 38 – Badge positioning

Jackets/blazers

If you are wearing a jacket, the badge can get hidden where it buttons up, even when the jacket is open. That is, if it is too low.

Check out Figure 39 – High and low badge position with two former business partners of mine: Dustin Hickle, on the left, and Muhammad Hutasuhut, on the right. Muhammad's badge is hidden by his jacket. Mine is positioned higher (see below for the how).

Yes, Muhammad was a good sport and allowed me to include this picture.

Figure 39 – High and low badge position

Meals – sitting at tables

When you are sitting down for a meal, a well-positioned badge is above the height of the table, so people can read it and reference it while engaging in conversation. This makes it easier for people to remember your name during the potential chaos of a meal (i.e., room noise, servers, etc.). It also makes them more comfortable.

How to Adjust your Badge?

- o Simply grab the top three inches of your lanyard and make a knot in it. If you have a collared shirt or jacket, tuck it neatly under the collar for a finished and professional look.
- o Some lanyards clip in at both sides of the badge at the top, so simply unclip one end and adjust your badge using the step above.

Badge Labels or Ribbons

To add them or not ... that is the question.

These can be viewed as "cheesy" or "cringy," so if you are unsure, take one or two when you are registering and apply them to your badge as you see fit (i.e., read the room).

Why?

- They are fun.
- They can make you stand out.
- They are a conversation piece.
- They may identify you as having a significant role in the event:
  - o Speaker
  - o Sponsor
  - o Chairperson

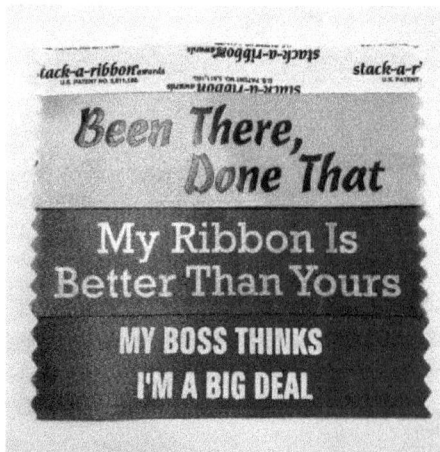

Figure 40 – Sample badge ribbons

Appendix G – Post-Event Report

Post-event reports are not only a good discipline, but they will inform the folks funding the event if it was worth it. It will also communicate the intangibles to decision-makers. This should be part of a regular cadence of communications.

This report is supported by the Event Budget Worksheet, the Return on Investment Worksheet and the Payback Period Worksheet.

Suggested cadence:

- One week after
  - The detailed post-event report is below
- Quarterly event summary
- Six months after should include Return on Event metrics in the quarterly event summary

Post-event report

Event name: [insert event name]
Date: [insert event date]
Location: [insert event location]
Report prepared by: [your name]
Date of report: [insert date]

1. Executive summary

Provide a brief overview of the trade show, including its purpose, key objectives, and a high-level summary of the results.

2. Event goals and objectives

- List key objectives such as brand awareness, lead generation, networking, product launch, etc.

- Measure success against each goal

3. Key metrics and performance indicators

Attendee engagement metrics:

- Total booth visitors: [insert number]

- Number of scheduled meetings: [insert number]

- Number of product demos conducted: [insert number]

- Attendee engagement duration (avg. time spent at booth): [insert time]

- QR code scans / business cards collected: [insert number]

Lead generation and sales metrics:

- Number of qualified leads: [insert number]

- Number of high-priority leads: [insert number]

- Conversion rate (leads to sales meetings booked): [insert %]

- Deals closed from the event: [insert number and revenue amount]

- Sales pipeline value from leads: [insert amount]

Marketing and brand awareness metrics:

- Social media mentions and engagement: [insert number]

- Press coverage and media mentions: [insert number]

- Website traffic increase during the event: [insert %]

- Number of promotional materials distributed: [insert number]

Return on Event (ROE) metrics:

- Total event budget: [insert amount]

- Cost per lead: [insert amount]

- Revenue generated from event-related sales: [insert amount]

- ROE calculation: [(Revenue - Cost) / Cost x 100%]

4. Competitor and market insights

- Summary of key competitors present and their activities

- Market trends observed during the event

- Feedback from attendees regarding competitor offerings

5. Attendee and customer feedback

- Summary of attendee feedback collected via surveys

- Common questions and concerns raised

- Testimonials and positive responses from visitors

6. Key learnings and recommendations

- What worked well?

- Challenges faced and areas for improvement

- Recommended actions for the next trade show

7. Next steps and follow-up actions

- Timeline for lead follow-up actions

- Assign responsibilities for nurturing leads

- Additional marketing activities post-event (email campaigns, social media, webinars)

Attachments and supporting documents:

- Lead list and contact details

- Photos from the event

- Copies of marketing materials used

Appendix H – Brand Ambassadors – Who Should You Take?

It is always interesting to pick your team. Here are some guidelines as you select your brand ambassadors to go to an event.

- How many people and why?
    - Size of event
    - Location/region
    - Size of booth/stand
- Location/region of event
    - Language
    - Travel costs
- Roles and skill sets
    - Executive and founder presence
    - Sales
    - Marketing
    - Solution engineer — demo guy or girl
- Relationships in market/industry
    - Will they bring value because they have been around the industry for a long time?
- Education
    - Do you have some young people or folks that are new to the industry that need to be introduced to other players in the industry?
    - Do these same people need to see how the veterans do it?
    - Learn from the industry elders
        - Emulate them early on and then make things your own.
        - Make an impact and see the connections between the past and the future.
        - They need new ideas and things to evolve, and you are in the right place, especially if you are 20 years younger than them.
- Attitudes
    - Will they show up?
        - In the morning, in the evening
        - Adhere to the dress code
        - Represent your brand with energy and consistency
    - Will they schedule pre-show meetings?

Appendix I – Sample Trade Show Booth Schedule

Day 1:

- 2:30 p.m. - 3:30 p.m.:
  - Set up booth
- 3:30 p.m. - 5:00 p.m.:
  - Networking (staff rotation for engaging with attendees)
- 5:00 p.m.:
  - Clean up booth and prepare for day 2
  - Remove all valuables — laptops, significant giveaway items or anything that can be easily stolen

Day 2:

- 7:30 a.m. - 8:00 a.m. (30 minutes before show opening: arrive at the venue, final booth preparations
- 8:00 a.m. - 5:00 p.m.:
  - Exhibit floor hours (staff rotation for working in the booth)
  - Morning: quick team meeting to review key points from the previous day and set objectives
  - Throughout the day: continue engaging with attendees, collecting leads and showcasing products
  - Lunch: rotate staff members for breaks to ensure coverage
  - Afternoon: focus on following up with potential leads and qualifying prospects
- 5:00 p.m. or at show closing time:
  - Break down booth
  - Pack boxes for shipping

Appendix J – Preparation at Home – Prior to Show

Two Weeks Out

You may need to do a few things that are not easy to do yourself, or it may take an appointment or an extra trip outside your home. Plan for these to feel confident and prepared.

- Dry cleaning
- Haircut
- Mani/pedi
- Acquire travel-size items you can bring in your carry-on luggage

Healthcare Items

Show floors are cold, drafty and dry. You will get thirsty, and your voice/throat will get hoarse from talking at an elevated volume over a few days — Tradeshow Throat. The change in climate or time zones and overall volume could also cause headaches. An outdoor event or lunch can be sunny; don't get burned, and bring sunglasses to avoid the squinting. You might not be able to find a shady spot at a table.

- Water bottle
- Advil/Tylenol
- Cough syrup / lozenges
- Sunscreen and sunglasses

What to Pack

This is very personal but there are a few things to consider.

- Climate and weather forecast
- Most conference rooms are kept on the cold side, so packing something that you can throw over your outfit is recommended
- Agenda of events
  - This may require a specific outfit if there is a theme
  - For example, bowling, a boat trip or a luau
- Comfort
  - You may do a lot of walking, so comfort might supersede style when it comes to shoes

Clothes

This list assumes a two-day event with a travel day ahead of the event.

Items	Men	Women
Shoes	Three pairs • Black • Brown • Running shoes (for your workout networking) Note: Wear your most comfortable pair of shoes to travel in • Flip-flops	Three pairs • Flats • Heels • Running shoes (for your workout networking) Note: Wear your most comfortable pair of shoes to travel in • Flip-flops
Pants	Three pairs of pants • Black • Other • Jeans (for after-hours events)	Three pairs of pants • Black • Other • Jeans (for after-hours events)
Shirts	Two dress shirts Three casual shirts or t-shirts	Two dress shirts or business tops Three casual shirts or t-shirts
Suits	One or two, depending on the event	One, depending on the event
Jackets	One jacket or cardigan	One jacket or cardigan
Workouts	Two workout outfits (shorts, t-shirts, socks)	Two workout outfits (shorts/leggings, t-shirts, socks)
Dresses/skirt		1 dress or skirt • Business Note: This could be replaced by a suit or vice-versa
Accessories (optional)	Watches/bracelets Ties Scarf Sunglasses	Watches Jewelry Scarf Sunglasses
Sleepwear	PJs	PJs
Underwear and socks	Five (this is personal, just trying to be comprehensive)	Five (this is personal, just trying to be comprehensive)

Appendix K – Lead Retrieval Application – Sample Questions

Exhibitors increasingly opt for trade show apps over traditional paper methods to gather lead data from in-booth interactions. Many trade shows offer lead retrieval apps for scanning badges, while some exhibitors invest in versatile lead capture software for multiple events.

Utilizing a trade show app streamlines data entry and export, saving valuable time. However, some exhibitors overlook the crucial step of incorporating qualifying questions into their digital lead capture process.

Customizing the app with company-specific qualifying questions requires time and effort, with uncertainty about whether booth staff will utilize them effectively. Yet, the benefits of obtaining answers to qualifying questions far outweigh the initial investment.

Crafting qualifying questions for trade show apps involves strategic considerations to advance business objectives and ensure practical utilization by booth staff.

Key considerations for crafting qualifying questions:

1. Keep the question list concise to ensure effective use by booth staff.

2. Focus on questions that aid sales prioritization and engagement and support marketing follow-up efforts.

3. Consult sales management for input on essential questions that define lead needs and qualification.

4. Prioritize questions that align with the BANT framework (Budget, Authority, Need, Time) but frame them in a non-intrusive manner to avoid deterring prospects.

5. Opt for multiple-choice answer formats whenever possible to facilitate easy response selection by booth staff and enable seamless integration with CRM systems for standardized lead evaluation and follow-up.

For instance, a question prompting the selection of the most suitable follow-up action allows booth staff to simultaneously assess lead quality and determine appropriate next steps.

- Questions
    I. What specific challenges are you hoping to address through solutions at this event?

II.   Do you have an XYZ product or solution?
- Competitive product #1
- Competitive product #2
- Competitive product #3
- Competitive product #4
- Other — space for details

III.   Are you happy with it?
- Yes
- No
- Space for details

IV.   Your value prop in the form of a question?
(e.g., Is it hard to maintain the product you are currently using? Are the internal users of the product happy with it?)
- Space for details

V.   Are you looking to make a change to any part of your tech stack or solution?
- Yes
- No
- Space for details

VI.   Has the project been budgeted for this year?
- Yes
- No
- Space for timeframe details

VII.   When do you want to have this project completed or implemented by?
- ASAP
- One month
- One quarter
- One year

VIII.   Is there a committee that is involved in the decision-making process? (These can be in a dropdown menu of your most common buying personas.)
- Role #1
- Role #2
- Role #3
- Other

IX.   Are there any functionalities you prioritize when evaluating products or services?
- Your top five functions in a dropdown menu
- Other — space for details

X.   When would be a good time to reach out to you to set up a more in-depth meeting and/or a demo?
- Next week
- 1-2 weeks from now
- 2-4 weeks from now
- Other — space for details

Sample output from an event

- Badge
- First Name
- Last Name
- Title
- Company
- Phone
- Email address
- Address Line 1
- Address Line 2
- City
- State
- ZIP
- Country
- Notes and output from questions

Other Qualification Questions

1. "How are you doing [x-workflow] right now, today?"
   - Ask this before you show a key workflow.
2. "How does this compare to how you're doing it now?"
   - Ask this after you show a key workflow.
3. "To what extent do you envision this being useful?"
   - Tonality matters on this one.
4. "How do you envision your team using this piece?"
   - Ask this to senior leaders who won't use your product.
5. "To what degree is this resonating so far with you?"
   - An easy way to make a question open-ended.
6. "To what extent do you see this solving [problem]?"
   - Puts the discussion closer to a pain point they shared earlier.
7. "What benefits do you see showing up in your world?"
   - Gets them voicing (and owning) the benefits.
8. "Where do you want to go deeper with questions?"
   - A pattern interrupt on "What questions do you have?"
9. "What challenge is going on that's making this resonate?"
   - Ask this after you strike a chord.
10. "Seems like that didn't resonate. Where'd I miss?"
    - Ask this when you think you've missed the mark.

Appendix L – Password Template

When you are at an event, more than one individual may be responsible for demonstrating your software, accessing the scanner or other password-protected tools. It is good to create and share a password sheet with your brand ambassadors, so everyone is prepared to deal with your booth visitors.

Password template

- **Length:** At least 10 characters (longer is better for security)

- **Format:**

    o   Two uppercase letters (A-Z)

    o   Two lowercase letters (a-z)

    o   Two numbers (0-9)

    o   Two special characters (!, @, #, $, %, etc.)

    o   Remaining characters: random mix of letters, numbers, and special characters

Device	Description	Password
SAMPLE	Demo device	WeDemoTheBest#1
Laptop 1	Demo device	
Scanner 1	Event badge scanner	
Tradeshow app	Event app	
Show list (Google sheet)	Internal	

The Pro Tips List

About the Author

Paul Abdool is a three-time vice president of sales and marketing and an author of books and articles. He learned about events and networking from his teenage years as a summer student setting up for multiple special events and trade shows throughout Canada. He also sold convention center space and decorating for a show company. His experience as an attendee, board member of associations, and event budget owner has helped him develop the know-how to ensure event success for his companies.

Along the way, mentors supported him by providing opportunities for him to attend conferences to watch them "net-work." He observed his mentors in action, researched the psychology of networking, and consistently practiced until he reached a level of comfort. He graduated from Wilfrid Laurier University with a B.A. in psychology and a diploma in business administration. He continues to practice networking daily and at events because he believes it is something we all need to keep working on.

The Origins of *From Workout to Last Call*

In this time of IRL (in real life) work making a comeback post-Covid, there was a bit of "rust" on both our event planning and networking skills. Our networking muscles began to atrophy into a little remote meeting square on our screens. Our marketing event budgets also shriveled up, and event and show planners began to struggle to make ends meet.

The Event Execution Section of *From Workout to Last Call* has been 40 years in development, from the time of making deliveries to convention centers for a summer job, to project managing events as a show decorator, to overseeing large budgets to sell booths to potential exhibitors, to ultimately deciding to attend and market my company's products and services as an exhibitor. I'm excited to share the ins and outs of the evolution of events, and the practical marketing and networking information that goes hand in hand with it.

The Networking Nexus Section of *From Workout to Last Call* is here to support you as you get back into "event and networking" shape. This book is for veteran event-goers and marketing teams, as well as recent graduates hitting the streets in the real world. It also addresses the fear of networking and the differences between interaction styles of extraverts, introverts and ambiverts.

www.ingramcontent.com/pod-product-compliance
Lightning Source LLC
Chambersburg PA
CBHW060930220326
41597CB00020BA/3460